Caroline Bigelow Le Row

Practical Recitations

Caroline Bigelow Le Row

Practical Recitations

ISBN/EAN: 9783337293857

Printed in Europe, USA, Canada, Australia, Japan

Cover: Foto ©Thomas Meinert / pixelio.de

More available books at **www.hansebooks.com**

Selections for Literary Exercises

APPROPRIATE FOR

RECEPTION-DAYS, HOLIDAYS, POETS' BIRTHDAYS, ETC.,

INCLUDING

CONCERT AND MUSICAL RECITATIONS, AND DIA-
LOGUES FROM POPULAR AUTHORS, ESPE-
CIALLY ARRANGED FOR THIS WORK.

BY

CAROLINE B. LeROW,

INSTRUCTOR IN ELOCUTION, CENTRAL SCHOOL, BROOKLYN, AND FORMERLY
INSTRUCTOR IN VASSAR AND SMITH COLLEGES.

NEW YORK:

CLARK & MAYNARD, PUBLISHERS,

771 BROADWAY AND 67 & 69 NINTH STREET.

PREFACE.

RECITATIONS form one of the most attractive features
of school entertainments, and give a pleasant variety to
every-day work ; yet few teachers have the time, even if
they have the ability, to drill pupils in the long and diffi-
cult pieces which form the bulk of the countless Recitations offered to the public.

The selections included in this volume are *in harmony
with the spirit of class-room work,* which demands brev-
ity, simplicity, good sense, and sound morality. This
is the only compilation of the kind in which these matters are considered as of equal importance with elocu-
tionary effect. Very few of the pieces are to be found
in any other book, and each one has been practically
tested in the school-room. The style of rendering,
wherever specified, can be changed, of course, to suit the
taste of the teacher.

As it is desirable that the largest possible number of
students should share in such exercises, many short
selections, excellent for practice in correct emphasis and
distinct articulation, are provided for the purpose.

The observance of our poets' birthdays is becoming a
pleasant and profitable custom in most schools, and

provision has been made for these anniversaries as well as for all other holidays.

As it is not possible to make liberal provision for each poet, it is hoped that the Alphabets will be suggestive of their best poems, and the prose extracts concerning the writers will inspire in students a desire to become better acquainted with them and their works.

CONTENTS.

Miscellaneous Recitations.

Concert Recitations.

Selections for Musical Accompaniment.

POETS' BIRTHDAYS.

William Cullen Bryant.

Contents.

Ralph Waldo Emerson.

Oliver Wendell Holmes.

Henry Wadsworth Longfellow.

James Russell Lowell.

John Greenleaf Whittier.

Contents.

LIST OF AUTHORS.

Practical Recitations.

MISCELLANEOUS SELECTIONS.

After Vacation.

Again they muster from the far-off hillside,
  From country farm-house and from sea-girt shore ;
Their tramping feet resound along the highways,
  Their gleeful shouts ring on the air once more.

A merry band, so full of youth's elixir,
  How can their restless spirits e'er essay
The tasks that wait their patient, steady labor
  After the long, bright, summer holiday?

Not now, O children, in the sunny meadows
  Ye cull the flowers or by the brooklets stray,
But in the fields of knowledge, thick with blossoms,
  To gather sweets for a far future day.

Here, too, you roam a land of fairest promise,
  Watered by many a stream of limpid hue,
Where weary travelers find a sweet refreshment
  And garner richest stores of old and new.

We bid thee welcome to the homes that missed thee,
  To the deserted school-room's open door.
The nation's hope is in thee, keep thy birthright;
  Thine heritage is more than golden store.

The Kingdom of Home.

THE PEOPLE'S HOLIDAYS.

MARIANNE FARNINGHAM.

NOT alone for the rich and great
    Are the beautiful works of God;
The mountain's slopes and the ocean's beach
    By the people's feet are trod,
And the poor man's children sing and dance
    On the green flower-covered sod.

Not alone for the cultured eyes
    Do the sweet flowers spring and grow;
There is scarcely living a man so poor
    But he may their sweetness know;
And out of the town to the fresh fair fields
    The toilers all can go.

Away from the factory shop and desk,
    Where the diligent work in throngs,
They go sometimes to the well-earned rest
    That to faithful zeal belongs ;
And the shore and the forest welcome them,
    And the larks pour down their songs.

" Man does not live by bread alone,"
    And well it needs must be
That we all should look on our Father's works
    By the river and lake and sea,
And spend our souls in adoring praise,
    For He careth for you and me.

And well may all with a stronger hand,
    And a braver, truer heart,
Go back to the task that God has given,
    And faithfully do our part ;
And bear in our souls the peace of the fields,
    To the counter, the desk, and the mart.

HOME LIGHTS.

THE light of June that shines on tremulous leaves
Of softest green, how fair a thing to see!
When shafts of dawn touch birch and maple tree,
Or sunset's hour a mesh of magic weaves;
The diamond light that flashes on the sea
In August noons,—a dazzle of pure rays.
With lovely ground of blue, whereon we gaze
From cliff or sandy shore in ecstasy;
The light that blazes on the mountain way,
Or, strained to pallor, steals to lonely dells;
None are forgotten on this autumn day,
As with sweet memories the glad heart swells;
But as the October sun drops down the west,
We say with smiling lips, Home lights are best.

CONCERNING BEGINNINGS AND ENDS.

REV. A. K. H. BOYD.

WE cannot bear a very long, uniform look-out. It is
an unspeakable blessing that we can stop and start again
in everything. The journey that crushes us down
when we contemplate it as one long weary thing can be
borne when we divide it into stages. And one great lesson of practical wisdom is to train ourselves to mentally
divide everything into stages. It would crush down any
man's resolution if he saw in one glance the whole enor-
mous bulk of labor which he will get through in a life-
time. And yet you know, and the little child knows
just as well, that after he has conquered that tremen-
dous alphabet, he must begin again with something else,
he must mount from his first little book onwards and
upwards into the fields of knowledge and learning. Let
us, if we are wise men, hold by the grand principle of
step by step.

A Strange Experience.

JOSEPHINE POLLARD.

THEY took the little London girl from out the city street
To where the grass was growing green, the birds were singing
    sweet;
And everything along the road so filled her with surprise,
The look of wonder fixed itself within her violet eyes.

The breezes ran to welcome her; they kissed her on each cheek,
And tried in every way they could their ecstasy to speak,
Inviting her to romp with them, and tumbling up her curls,
Expecting she would laugh or scold, like other little girls.

But she did not; no, she could not; for this crippled little
    child
Had lived within a dingy court where sunshine never smiled,
And for weary, weary days and months the little one had lain
Confined within a narrow room, and on a couch of pain.

The out-door world was strange to her—the broad expanse of
    sky,
The soft, green grass, the pretty flowers, the stream that
    trickled by;
But all at once she saw a sight that made her hold her breath,
And shake and tremble as if she were frightened near to death.

Oh, like some horrid monster of which the child had dreamed,
With nodding head and waving arms, the angry creature
    seemed;
It threatened her, it mocked at her, with gestures and grimace
That made her shrink with terror from its serpent-like em-
    brace.

They kissed the trembling little one, they held her in their
    arms,
And tried in every way they could to quiet her alarms,
And said, "Oh, what a foolish little goose you are to be
So nervous and so terrified at nothing but a tree!"

They made her go up close to it, and put her arms around
The trunk and see how firmly it was fastened in the ground;
They told her all about the roots that clung down deeper yet,
And spoke of other curious things she never would forget.

Oh, I have heard of many, very many girls and boys
Who have to do without the sight of pretty books and toys,
Who have never seen the ocean; but the saddest thought to me
Is that anywhere there lives a child who never saw a tree.

THE DAILY TASK.

MARIANNE FARNINGHAM.

THE morning light falls gently on the eyes
    And wakes the sleeping men;
And bids them rise and haste to meet the day,
    And find their work again.

No one is asked to choose what he will do,
    Or take the task loved best,
For God allots the places, and each one
    Obeys His high behest.

One, loving silence, passes to the street
    And mingles with the crowd,
And finds his daily work awaiting him,
    Where noise is long and loud.

And one who hungers for the voice and touch
    Of others in the gloom
Is ordered to withdraw from all, and work
    Alone within one room.

Another, loving beauty, air, and light,
    Passes in sordid ways,
And uncongenial sights, and jarring sounds,
    The hours of his best days.

And yet another who could love all work,
   And do it thankfully,
Has naught to do but suffer and be still
   In patience, perfectly.

Are, then, the workers at their daily tasks
   Unhappy and unblest?
Nay; He who chooses for them gives the wage
   Of happiness and rest.

The feet pass swiftly to the place of toil,
   The lips break into song,
And ready hands receive the allotted task,
   Nor find the hours too long.

Because the loyal heart is true to God,
   And the deft hand obeys
The Master, who decides what each shall do,
   Joy fills the working days.

And so, if but the soul be leal, the task
   Itself becomes more dear,
And every worker finds that work well done
   Is work that brings good cheer.

"WHAT'S THE LESSON FOR TO-DAY?"

LITTLE Bess, with laughing eyes,
Brightly blue as summer skies,
Came to me one morn in May,
Asking in her eager way,
" What's the lesson for to-day?"

And I told her, then and there,
What I wished her to prepare.
But new meaning (strange to say),
In the childish query lay,
" What's the lesson for to-day?"

And I pondered o'er and o'er
What I scarce had thought before,—
As I went my wonted way,
Towards my duty, sad or gay,
" What's *my* lesson for the day ?"

Students in the school of life,
'Mid its struggles and its strife,
Let *us* ask, in childlike way,
Of the Teacher we obey,
" What's the lesson for to-day ?"

And the answer God will give,
He will show us how to live,
Teach us of His perfect way,
Grant us wisdom that we may
Learn the lesson of the day.

MORAL COURAGE.

REV. SYDNEY SMITH.

A GREAT deal of talent is lost in the world for the want
of a little courage.   The fact is, that to do anything in
this world worth doing, we must not stand back shivering, and thinking of the cold and the danger, but jump
in and scramble through as well as we can.   It will not
do to be perpetually calculating tasks, and adjusting
nice chances ; it did very well before the flood, where a
man could consult his friends upon an intended publi-
cation for an hundred and fifty years, and then live to
see its success afterwards : but at present, a man waits
and doubts and hesitates, and consults his brother and
his uncle and particular friends, till one fine day he
finds that he is sixty years of age ; that he has lost so
much time in consulting his first cousin and particular
friends, that he has no more time to follow their advice.

No Work the Hardest Work.

CHARLES F. ORNE.

Ho! ye who at the anvil toil,
  And strike the sounding blow,
Where from the burning iron's breast
  The sparks fly to and fro,
While answering to the hammer's ring,
  And fire's intenser glow—
Oh, while ye feel 'tis hard to toil
  And sweat the long day through,
Remember it is harder still
  To have no work to do.

Ho! ye who till the stubborn soil,
  Whose hard hands guide the plow;
Who bend beneath the summer sun
  With burning cheek and brow—
Ye deem the curse still clings to earth
  From olden time till now;
But while ye feel 'tis hard to toil
  And labor all day through,
Remember it is harder still
  To have no work to do.

Ho! ye who plow the sea's blue field,
  Who ride the restless wave;
Beneath whose gallant vessel's keel
  There lies a yawning grave;
Around whose bark the wintry winds
  Like fiends of fury rave—
Oh, while ye feel 'tis hard to toil
  And labor long hours through,
Remember it is harder still
  To have no work to do.

Ho! all who labor, all who strive,
  Ye wield a mighty power;
Do with your might, do with your strength,
  Fill every golden hour;

The glorious privilege to do
  Is man's most noble dower.
Oh, to your birthright and yourselves.
  To your own souls be true!
A weary, wretched life is theirs
  Who have no work to do.

———◆———

SOME OLD SCHOOL-BOOKS.

I HAVE been back to my home again,
  To the place where I was born;
I have heard the wind from the stormy main
  Go rustling through the corn;
I have seen the purple hills once more;
  I have stood on the rocky coast
Where the waves storm inland to the shore;
  But the thing that touched me most

Was a little leather strap that kept
  Some school-books, tattered and torn!
I sighed, I smiled, I could have wept
  When I came on them one morn;
For I thought of the merry little lad,
  In the mornings sweet and cool,
If weather was good, or weather bad,
  Going whistling off to school.

My fingers undid the strap again,
  And I thought how my hand had changed,
And half in longing, and half in pain,
  Backward my memory ranged.
There was the grammar I knew so well,—
  I didn't remember a rule;
And the old blue speller,—I used to spell
  Better than any in school;

And the wonderful geography
  I've read on the green hill-side,
When I've told myself I'd surely see
  All lands in the world so wide,
From the Indian homes in the far, far West,
  To the mystical Cathay.
I have seen them all.   But Home is best
  When the evening shades fall gray.

And there was the old arithmetic,
  All tattered and stained with tears;
I and Jamie and little Dick
  Were together in by-gone years.
Jamie has gone to the better land;
  And I get now and again,
A letter in Dick's bold, ready hand,
  From some great Western plain.

There wasn't a book, and scarce a page,
  That hadn't some memory
Of days that seemed like a golden age,
  Of friends I shall no more see.
And so I picked up the books again
  And buckled the strap once more,
And brought them over the tossing main;
  Come, children, and look them o'er.

And there they lie on a little stand
  Not far from the Holy Book;
And his boys and girls with loving care
  O'er grammar and speller look.
He said, "They speak to me, children dear,
  Of a past without alloy;
And the look of Books, in promise clear,
  Of a future full of joy."

Harper's Weekly.

THEIR COST.

ELLEN M. H. GATES.

How cheap are the things which are bought and sold,
The beautiful things which the hands can hold,
Whatever is purchased with silver and gold.

The merchants are calling and filling their rooms
With jewels and laces and rarest perfumes,
And wonderful webs from the Indian looms.

The price of the treasures is small, as they say;
For dollars and cents, are exchanged every day
The furs of the North-land, the silks of Cathay.

But, oh! the rare things which can never be brought
From the far-away countries, but still must be sought
Through working and waiting and anguish of thought!

The patience that comes to the heart, as it tries
To hear, through all discord and turbulent cries,
The songs of the armies that march to the skies;

The courage that fails not, nor loses its breath
In stress of the battle, but smilingly saith,
" I'll measure my strength with disaster and death;"

The love that through doubting and pain will increase;
The longing and restlessness, calmed into peace
That is perfect and satisfied, never to cease—

These, these are the dear things. No king on his throne
Can buy them away from the poor and unknown
Who make them, through labor or anguish, their own.

A TRUE life must be simple in all its elements.—HOR-
ACE GREELEY.

THE OLD READING CLASS.

WILL CARLETON.

I.

I CANNOT tell you, Genevieve, how oft it comes to me—
That rather young old reading class in District Number Three,
That row of elocutionists who stood so straight in line,
And charged at standard literature with amiable design.
We did not spare the energy in which our words were clad!
We gave the meaning of the text by all the light we had;
But still I fear the ones who wrote the lines we read so free
Would scarce have recognized their work in District Number
    Three.

II.

Outside, the snow was smooth and clean—the winter's thick-
    laid dust;
The storm, it made the windows speak at every sudden gust;
Bright sleigh-bells threw us pleasant words when travelers
    would pass;
The maple-trees along the road stood shivering in their class;
Beyond, the white-browed cottages were nestling cold and
    dumb,
And far away the mighty world seemed beckoning us to come—
The wondrous world, of which we conned what had been and
    might be,
In that old-fashioned reading class of District Number Three.

III.

We took a hand at History—its altars, spires and flames—
And uniformly mispronounced the most important names;
We wandered through Biography, and gave our fancy play,
And with some subjects fell in love—"good only for one
    day;"
In Romance and Philosophy we settled many a point,
And made what poems we assailed to creak at every joint;
And many authors that we love, you with me will agree,
Were first time introduced to us in District Number Three.

IV.

You recollect Susannah Smith, the teacher's sore distress,
Who never stopped at any pause—a sort of day express ?
And timid young Sylvester Jones, of inconsistent sight,
Who stumbled on the easy words and read the hard ones right?
And Jennie Green, whose doleful voice was always clothed in
    black ?
And Samuel Hicks, whose tones induced the plastering all to
    . crack ?
And Andrew Tubbs, whose various mouths were quite a show
    to see ?
Alas! we cannot find them now in District Number Three.

V.

And Jasper Jenckes, whose tears would flow at each pathetic
    word
(He's in the prize-fight business now, and hits them hard, I've
    heard);
And Benny Bayne, whose every tone he murmured as in fear
(His tongue is not so timid now: he is an auctioneer);
And Lanty Wood, whose voice was just endeavoring hard to '
    change,
And leaped from hoarse to fiercely shrill with most surprising
    range;
Also his sister Mary Jane, so full of prudish glee.
Alas! they're both in higher schools than District Number
    Three.

VI.

So back these various voices come, though long the years have
    grown,
And sound uncommonly distinct through Memory's telephone;
And some are full of melody, and bring a sense of cheer,
And some can smite the rock of time, and summon forth a tear;
But one sweet voice comes back to me, whenever sad I grieve!
And sings a song, and that is yours, O peerless Genevieve!
It brightens up the olden times, and throws a smile at me—
A silver star amid the clouds of District Number Three.

FORWARD.

SUSAN COOLIDGE.

LET me stand still upon the height of life;
  Much has been won, though much there is to win;
I am a little weary of the strife.
  Let me stand still awhile, nor count it sin
To cool my hot brow, ease the travel-pain,
And then address me to the road again.

Long was the way, and steep and hard the climb;
  Sore are my limbs, and fain I am to rest;
Behind me lie long sandy tracks of time;
  Before me rises the steep mountain crest.
Let me stand still; the journey is half done,
And when less weary I will travel on.

There is no standing still! Even as I pause
  The steep path shifts and I slip back apace;
Movement was safety; by the journey laws
  No help is given, no safe abiding-place,
No idling in the pathway hard and slow;
I must go forward, or must backward go!

I will go up then, though the limbs may tire,
  And though the path be doubtful and unseen;
Better with the last effort to expire
  Than lose the toil and struggle that have been,
And have the morning strength, the upward strain,
The distance conquered, in the end made vain.

Ah, blessed law! for rest is tempting sweet,
  And we would all lie down if so we might;
And few would struggle on with b' ..'ling feet ;
  And few would ever gain the h'gher height
Except for the stern law which bids us know
We must go forward, or must backward go.

HER ANGEL.

ANNA F. BURNHAM.

MARGERY cowered and crouched in the door of the beautiful
porch.
There were beautiful people in there, and they all belonged to
the church.
But Margery waited without; she did not belong anywhere
Except in the dear Lord's bosom, who taketh the children there.

And through the open doorway came floating a lovely sound;
She shut her eyes and imagined how the angels stood around
With their harps like St. Cecilia's in the picture on the wall—
Ah, Margery did not doubt that so looked the singers all.

" Suffer the little children!" sang a heavenly voice somewhere,
Or the soul of a voice that was winging away in the upper air;
" Let the children come to me!" sang the angel in her place,
And Margery, listening, stood, with upturned eyes and face.

"Let them come! let them come to me!" And up the aisle
she sped
With eyes that sought for the Voice, to follow where it led.
She did not say to herself: "I'm coming! Wait for me!"
But it shone in her face, and it leaped in her eyes, dear Margery!

Up the stair to the singer she ran, she touched the hem of her
dress.
But the choir were bending their heads, the preacher had
risen to bless
The reverent throng, and alas! bewildered Margery,
The Voice has ceased, and the singers have turned their eyes
on thee.

They look with surprise at her feet, and again at her ragged
gown,
And one by one they pass with a careless smile or a frown;
But the sweetest face bent near, and—" I came," said Margery,
" For I thought 'twas an angel sang, 'Let the children come
to me!'"

With a tender sigh the singer took the child upon her knee;
"I sang the words for the dear Lord Christ, my Margery,
And so, for the dear Lord Christ, I take thee home with me!
—"It was an angel sang!" sobs little Margery.

ARE THE HEROES DEAD?

HELEN LEE SARGENT.

"WE are low,—we are base!" sigh the singers,
 "The heroes have long been dead!
The times have fallen,—the state is sick,
 And the glory of earth has fled!
Sordid and selfish on every side
 Walk the men and the women we know.
Downward we tend continually,
 And faster and faster go!"

Shame to ye, shame to ye, singers!
 And have ye never known
That the soul of man has been ever the same
 Since the sun of heaven shone?
If ye listen and look for the heroes,
 Ye will find them everywhere;
But if ye look for the knaves and scamps—
 It is true they are not rare.

But whenever a ship is lost at sea,
 Or a building burns on land,
Amid the terror and death and loss
 A hero is found at hand.
And if ever a war should come again
 (From it long may we be freed!)
Ye will find the heroes, as ever before,
 Responding to the need.

FAILED!

A POEM OF HARD TIMES.

PHILLIPS THOMPSON.

FAILED! Jim Miserton failed! You don't mean to say it's so?
Had it from Smith at the Bank? Well, he's a man that should
   know.
Forty-two cents on the dollar? I cannot believe my ears.
There's no such thing as judging a man by the way he appears.

Yes, you may well say "failed;" there's more than the term
   implies,
When all there is of a man in a hopeless ruin lies.
To come after twenty years of a stubborn up-hill strife,
It isn't a business smash so much as a failure in life.

Gold was always his god—he'd nothing else in his soul;
Money, for money's sake, was ever his ultimate goal.
A "self-made man" they styled him, for low and poor he be-
   gan;
But now his money has vanished, and what is left of the man?

He had no eye for beauty, for literature no taste;
Buying pictures or books he counted a shameful waste.
Nothing he cared for art or the poet's elaborate rhymes;
His soul was only attuned to the musical jingle of dimes.

Selfish, exacting, and stern, a hand he would treat like a
   slave;
Long were his hours of toil, and scanty the pay that he gave ;
Made of cast-iron himself, his zeal in the struggle for gold
Left him no pity to spare for those of a different mold.

Never a cent for the poor, for the naked never a stitch;
'Twas all their fault, he would say; they should save like him,
   and grow rich.
Now and then to a church he'd forward a liberal amount,
Duly set down in his books to the advertising account.

So he succeeded, of course, and piled his coffers with wealth,
Missing pleasure and culture, losing vigor and health;
Now he's down at the bottom, exactly where he began;
Even his gold has vanished, and what is left of the man?

A self-made man, indeed! then we owe no honor to such;
The genuine self-made man you cannot honor too much;
But be sure what you make *is* a man—with a heart, and a
    soul, and a mind,
Not merely a pile of dollars, that goes, leaving nothing behind.

——◆——

LABOR.

REV. ORVILLE DEWEY.

To *some* field of labor, mental or manual, every idler
should fasten, as a chosen and coveted theater of im-
provement.   But so he is not impelled to do, under the
teachings of our imperfect civilization.   On the contrary,
he sits down, folds his hands, and blesses himself in his
idleness.   This way of thinking is the heritage of the
absurd and unjust feudal system under which serfs la-
bored, and gentlemen spent their lives in fighting and
feasting.   It is time that this opprobrium of toil were
done away.   Ashamed to toil, art thou?   Ashamed of
thy dingy work-shop and dusty labor-field; of thy hard
hand scarred with service more honorable than that of
war; of thy soiled and weather-stained garments, on
which Mother Nature has embroidered, midst sun and
rain, midst fire and steam, her own heraldic honors?
Ashamed of these tokens and titles, and envious of the
flaunting robes of imbecile idleness and vanity?   It is
treason to nature; it is impiety to Heaven; it is breaking Heaven's great ordinance.   TOIL, I repeat—*toil*,
either of the brain, of the heart, or of the hand, is the
only true manhood, the only true nobility.

THE HOLY PLACE.

MARY FRANCES BUTTS.

THE people came to the priest,
  " Good father," said they,
" We love the holy altar
    Where we kneel to pray;
We would 'broider a cloth
    Of fine silk and wool
To cover the altar,
    For our hearts are full."

" My children," said the priest,
  " When the heart is full,
Spend not its treasure
    In fine silk and wool.
Listen, my children,
    Do you hear a moan?
'Tis the poor man waiting,
    Sick and alone.

" His darlings ask in vain
    For a piece of bread;
And what thinks the Lord?"
    The good priest said.
" The tender-hearted Christ
    Would be very wroth
Should you leave his poor
    For an altar-cloth.

" He blesses the holy altar
    Where we kneel to pray;
But in the silence
    I hear him say:
" Seek me, my children,
    In works of grace;
Where you comfort a heart
    Is the holy place."

A DISCOURSE OF BUDDHA.

EDWIN ARNOLD.

HEREWITH a broken beam of Buddha's lore,
One raylet of his glorious gift of light,
Rose-gleam which lingers when the sun is down
Such space that men may find a path thereby.
          A priest questioned him:
" ' Which is Life's chief good, Master ? '   And he spake:

" ' Shadows are good, when the high sun is flaming,
    From whereso'er they fall;
 Some take their rest beneath the holy temple,
    Some by the prison wall.

" ' The king's gilt palace roof shuts off the sunlight,
    So doth the dyer's shed!
 Which is the chiefest shade of all the shadows ? '
    ' They are alike! ' one said.

" ' So is it,' quoth he, ' with all shows or living;
    As shadows fall, they fall!
 Rest under, if ye must, but question not
    Which is the best of all.

" ' Yet in the forest some trees wave with fragrance
    Of fruit and bloom o'erhead;
 And some are evil, bearing fruitless branches
    Whence poisonous air is spread.

" ' Therefore, though all be shows, seek, if ye must,
    Right shelter from life's heat;
 Lo! these do well who toil for wife and child
    Threading the burning street.

" ' Good is it helping kindred! good to dwell
    Blameless and just to all;
 Good to give alms, with good-will in the heart,
    Albeit the store be small!

" ' Good to speak sweet and gentle words, to be
    Merciful, patient, and mild;
To hear the law and keep it, leading days
    Innocent, undefiled.

" ' These the chief goods—for evil by its like
    Ends not, nor hate by hate;
By love hate ceaseth, by well-doing ill,
    By knowledge life's dark state.

" ' Look! yonder soars an eagle! mark those wings
    Which cleave the blue, cool skies!
What shadow needeth that proud Lord of Air
    To shield his fearless eyes?

" ' Rise from this life! lift upon new-spread pinions
    Heart free and great as his!
The eagle seeks no shadow, nor the wise
    Greater or lesser bliss! ' "

———◆———

WE are unwilling walkers. We are not innocent and
simple-hearted enough to enjoy a walk. We have fallen
from that state of grace which capacity to enjoy a walk
implies. It cannot be said that as a people we are so
positively sad or morose as that we are vacant of that
sportiveness of animal spirits that characterized our ancestors, and that springs from full and harmonious life,
—a sound heart in accord with a sound body. A man
must invest himself near at hand, and in common things,
and be content with a steady and moderate return, if he
would know the blessedness of a cheerful heart, and the
sweetness of a walk over the round earth. This is a lesson the American has yet to learn,—capability of amuse-
ment on a low key.—JOHN BURROUGHS.

To FILL the youthful mind with lofty and noble ideas, to stock the memory with the richest vocabulary, and to acquire a wide command of our grand English language, we have nothing better, except the Bible, than the plays of Shakespeare.

Extracts from Shakespeare once thoroughly committed to memory are never forgotten. Many of the world's great orators and statesmen were wont to commit and recite passages from Shakespeare. Edmund Burke made Shakespeare his daily study, while Erskine, it is said, could have held conversation on every subject in the phrases of the great dramatist. Rufus Choate was familiar with every line of Shakespeare. Daniel Webster never tired of repeating passages from the same author. The genial Dr. Holmes tells us that Wendell Phillips, Motley the historian, and himself, when boys, used to declaim Antony's oration on holiday afternoons over the prostrate form of some younger playmate.

SPARROWS.

ADELINE D. T. WHITNEY.

LITTLE birds sit on the telegraph wires,
　　And chitter and flitter and fold their wings.
Maybe they think that for them and their sires
　　Stretched always on purpose, those wonderful strings;
And perhaps the thought that the world inspires
　　Did plan for the birds among other things.

Little birds sit on the slender lines,
　　And the news of the world runs under their feet:
How value rises and now declines,
　　How kings with their armies in battle meet;
And all the while, 'mid the soundless signs,
　　They chirp their small gossipings, foolish and sweet.

Little things light on the lines of our lives—
Hopes and joys and acts of to-day;
And we think that for these the Lord contrives,
Nor catch what the hidden lightnings say;
Yet from end to end his meaning arrives,
And his word runs underneath all the way.

Is life only wires and lightning, then,
Apart from that which about it clings?
Are the thoughts and the works and the prayers of men
Only sparrows that light on God's telegraph strings—
Holding a moment and gone again?
Nay: he planned for the birds with the larger things!

—————•—————

But, above all, where thou findest ignorance, stupidity, brute-mindedness—attack it, I say ; smite it wisely, unweariedly, and rest not while thou livest and it lives ; but smite, smite in the name of God ! The highest God, as I understand it, does audibly so command thee : still audibly, if thou have ears to hear. He, even He, with his unspoken voice, is fuller than any Sinai thunders, or syllabled speech of whirlwinds ; for the SILENCE of deep eternities, of worlds beyond the morning stars, does it not speak to thee? The unborn ages; the old graves, with their long moldering dust, the very tears that wetted it, now all dry—do not these speak to thee what ear hath not heard? The deep death-kingdoms, the stars in their never-resting courses, all space and all time, proclaim it to thee in continual silent admonition. Thou, too, if ever man should, shalt work while it is called to-day; for the night cometh, wherein no man can work.—THOMAS CARLYLE.

3

THE STORMING OF STONY POINT.

(July 16, 1779.)

ELAINE GOODALE.

THE wonder of midnight, now pregnant with wars,
Skies mellow and fruitful, all trembling with stars,
The ripe, yellow planet, poised low in the west,
The smooth-flowing river, with stars on its breast;
      These murmur of Wayne,
      Mad Anthony Wayne,—
He has life-blood to lose, he has glory to gain!

The low-lying marshes, where, silent and stern,
Twelve hundred are creeping through bog-grass and fern,
With fireflies for lanterns; while, black-throated still,
The cannon are cold in the fort on the hill,—
      These whisper of Wayne,
      Mad Anthony Wayne,
Every sense up in arms, every nerve on the strain.

The noiseless approach, and the desperate close;
The flash of the steel, and the blood as it flows;
The hero, once wounded, who cries,—"I shall win!
Let me die in the fort! Men, carry me in!"
      These tell us of Wayne,
      Mad Anthony Wayne,
With nerves hard as iron, despising the pain!

The red flag of morning, displayed in the skies,
Brings a stern look of joy to the conqueror's eyes,—
Those eyes that flashed full on his chief (so they tell),—
"What! storm Stony Point? You may bid me storm hell!"
      We'll believe it of Wayne,
      Mad Anthony Wayne,
The bravest of foes, and the peer of his slain!

HUMILITY.

ERNEST W. SHURTLEFF.

SWEET are the roses in the pasture lane,
   Like flakes of sunset dropped from some rich cloud—
Oh, sweet, indeed, but not with sweetness vain;
   Nor is the pasture of their presence proud.
Not for themselves they blossom, bud and nod—
They spring to breathe to man the peace of God.

I never heard a songster's lay that told
   Of aught but simple joy and grateful praise.
The oriole, with throat aflame with gold,
   Dreams not he is a charm to mortal gaze;
No bird to laud himself hath ever sung—
His song is for the flowers he chirps among.

The sun that fills the skies with summer calms,
   The stars that light unmeasured depths of space
Like distant suns that flash reflected charms,
   When on the night Jehovah turns his face—
All these in humbleness their glory wear,
Grateful, not proud, because Heaven made them fair.

O vaunting man, go ponder on these things!
   Think—what is glory in thy Maker's view?
Who wins the passing praise the cold world sings
   Not always earns the praise of Heaven too.
Thou mayst through life thy name with gods enroll,
Yet bear rebuke of angels in thy soul.

Oh, to be simple in the lives we lead!
   To know that what we hold is not our own!
The lily is as modest as the weed,
   The mountain humble as the broken stone.
Since man is proud, how wise it is, how just,
That death should come to teach us we are dust!

WHAT OF THAT?

TIRED? Well, what of that?
Didst fancy life was spent on beds of ease,
Fluttering the rose-leaves scattered by the breeze?
Come, rouse thee! work while it is called day!
Coward, arise! go forth upon thy way.

Lonely? And what of that?
Some must be lonely; 'tis not given to all
To feel a heart responsive rise and fall,
To blend another life into its own;
Work may be done in loneliness. Work on!

Dark? Well, and what of that?
Didst fondly dream the sun would never set?
Dost fear to lose thy way? Take courage yet.
Learn thou to walk by faith, and not by sight;
Thy steps will guided be, and guided right.

Hard? Well, what of that?
Didst fancy life one summer holiday,
With lessons none to learn, and naught but play?
Go, get thee to thy task! Conquer or die!
It must be learned; learn it, then, patiently.

———◆———

KNOWLEDGE has in our time triumphed, and is still triumphing, over prejudice and over bigotry. The civilized and Christian world is fast learning the great lesson that difference of nation does not imply necessary hostility, and that all contact need not be war. The whole world is becoming a common field for intellect to act in. Energy of mind, genius, power, wheresoever it exists, may speak out in any tongue, and the world will hear it.—DANIEL WEBSTER.

THE OLD FOLKS IN THE NEW SCHOOL-HOUSE.

THINGS ain't now as they used to be
    A hundred years ago,
When schools were kept in private rooms
    Above stairs or below;
When sturdy boys and rosy girls
    Romped through the drifted snow,
And spelled their duty and their "abs,"
    A hundred years ago.

Those old school-rooms were dark and cold
    When winter's sun ran low;
But darker was the master's frown,
    A hundred years ago;
And high hung up the birchen rod,
    That all the school might see,
Which taught the boys obedience
    As well as Rule of Three.

Though 'twas but little that they learned,
    A hundred years ago,
Yet what they got they ne'er let slip,—
    'Twas well whipped in, you know.
But now the times are greatly changed,
    The rod has had its day,
The boys are won by gentle words,
    And girls by love obey.

The school-house now a palace is,
    And scholars, kings and queens;
They master Algebra and Greek
    Before they reach their teens.
Where once was crying, music sweet
    Her soothing influence sheds;
Ferules are used for beating time,
    And not for beating heads.

Yes, learning was a ragged boy,
    A hundred years ago;
With six weeks schooling in a year,
    What could the urchin do?
But now he is a full-grown man,
    And boasts attainments rare;
He's got his silver slippers on,
    And running everywhere.

THE BARBAROUS CHIEF.

ELLA WHEELER WILCOX.

THERE was a kingdom known as the Mind,
    A kingdom vast, as fair,
And the brave King Brain had the right to reign
    In royal splendor there.
Oh! that was a beautiful, beautiful land
    Which unto this king was given;
It was filled with everything good and grand,
    And it reached from earth to heaven.

But a savage monster came one day,
    From over a distant border;
He made war on the king and usurped his sway,
    And set everything in disorder.
He mounted the throne, which he made his own,
    And the kingdom was sunk in grief,
There was sorrow and shame from the hour he came—
    Ill Temper, the barbarous chief.

He threw down the castles of Love and Peace,
    He burned up the altars of prayers;
He trod down the grain that was sowed by Brain,
    And planted thistles and tares.
He wasted the storehouse of knowledge, and drove
    Queen Wisdom away in fright,
And a terrible gloom like the cloud of doom
    Shadowed that land with night.

Then, bent on more havoc, away he rushed
　To the neighboring kingdom Heart,
And the blossoms of kindness and hope he crushed,
　And patience was made to depart.
And he even went on to the isthmus Soul,
　That unites the Mind with God,
And its beautiful bowers and fragrant flowers
　With a reckless heel he trod.

Oh ! to you is given this beautiful land
　Where the lordly Brain has sway—
But the border ruffian is near at hand—
　And be on your guard, I pray.
Beware of *Ill Temper*, the barbarous chief,
　He is cruel as Vice or Sin;
He will certainly bring your kingdom grief,
　If once you let him in.

GROWTH.

HORACE MANN.

AT first the mind cannot project itself outward, if
we may so speak, even so far as the eye can reach.
A child may see with the eye the outlines of a distant
mountain long before his mind can, as it were, leap
over the intervening space. But soon the mind attains
a power of flight compared with which the space
traveled by the keenest eye, aided by the best telescope,
is nothing. The eye, indeed, can see the remote star,
whose light, traveling since its creation at the rate of
two hundred thousand miles a second, has but just
reached the earth; but all this is only a hand-breadth
compared with the depths in the abysses of space into
which the adventurous mind plunges itself.

A BIRD'S MINISTRY.

MARGARET J. PRESTON.

FROM his home in an eastern bungalow,
In sight of the everlasting snow
Of the grand Himalayas, row on row,
Thus wrote my friend:

                    "I had traveled far
From the Afghan towers of Candahar,
Through the sand-white plains of Sinde-Sagar;

"And once, when the daily march was o'er,
As tired I sat in my tented door,
Hope failed me, as never it failed before.

"In swarming city, at wayside fane,
By the Indus' bank, on the scorching plain,
I had taught,—and my teaching all seemed vain.

"'No glimmer of light [I sighed] appears;
The Moslem's fate and the Buddhist's fears
Have gloomed their worship this thousand years.

"'For Christ and His truth I stand alone
In the midst of millions; a sand-grain blown
Against yon temple of ancient stone.

"'As soon may level it!' Faith forsook
My soul, as I turned on the pile to look;
Then rising, my saddened way I took

"To its lofty roof, for the cooler air;
I gazed, and marveled;—how crumbled were
The walls I had deemed so firm and fair!

"For, wedged in a rift of the massive stone,
Most plainly rent by its roots alone,
A beautiful peepul-tree had grown;

" Whose gradual stress would still expand
The crevice, and topple upon the sand
The temple, while o'er its work would stand

" The tree in its living verdure !—Who
Could compass the thought ?—The bird that flew
Hitherward, dropping a seed that grew,

" Did more to shiver this ancient wall
Than earthquake,—war,—simoon,—or all
The centuries, in their lapse and fall !

" Then I knelt by the riven granite there,
And my soul shook off its weight of care,
As my voice rose clear on the tropic air:

" ' The living seeds I have dropped remain
In the cleft; Lord, quicken with dew and rain,
Then temple and mosque shall be rent in twain !' "

EXTRACT FROM A LETTER.

WILLIAM WIRT.

I WANT to tell you a secret. The way to make yourself pleasing to others, is to show that you care for them.
The world is like the miller at Mansfield, " who cared for
nobody, no, not he, because nobody cared for him."
And the whole world will serve you so if you give them
the same cause. Let every one, therefore, see that you
do care for them, by showing them what Sterne so hap-
pily calls " the small, sweet courtesies," in which there is
no parade ; whose voice is to still, to ease; and which
manifest themselves by tender and affectionate looks
and little kind acts of attention, giving others the pref-
erence in every little enjoyment at the table, in the field,
walking, sitting, or standing.

THE COAST-GUARD.

EMILY HUNTINGTON MILLER.

Do you wonder what I am seeing,
  In the heart of the fire, aglow
Like cliffs in a golden sunset,
  With a summer sea below?
I see, away to the eastward,
  The line of a storm-beat coast,
And I hear the tread of the hurrying waves
  Like the tramp of the mailèd host.

And up and down in the darkness,
  And over the frozen sand,
I hear the men of the coast-guard
  Pacing along the strand,
Beaten by storm and tempest,
  And drenched by the pelting rain,
From the shores of Carolina
  To the wind-swept bays of Maine.

No matter what storms are raging,
  No matter how wild the night,
The gleam of their swinging lanterns
  Shines out with a friendly light.
And many a shipwrecked sailor
  Thanks God, with his gasping breath,
For the sturdy arms of the surfmen
  That drew him away from death.

And so, when the wind is wailing,
  And the air grows dim with sleet,
I think of the fearless watchers
  Pacing along their beat.
I think of a wreck, fast breaking
  In the surf of a rocky shore,
And the life-boat leaping onward
  To the stroke of the bending oar.

I hear the shouts of the sailors,
　The boom of the frozen sail,
And the creak of the icy halyards
　Straining against the gale.
" Courage !" the captain trumpets,
　" They are sending help from land !"
God bless the men of the coast-guard,
　And hold their lives in His hand !

A Turkish Tradition.

'Tis said the Turk, when passing down
　An Eastern street,
If any scrap of paper chance
　His eyes to greet,

Will never look away, like us,
　Unheedingly,
Or pass the little fragment thus
　Regardless by,

But stop to pick it up because,
　Oh, lovely thought !
The name of God may thereupon
　Perchance be wrought.

In every human soul remains,
　However dim,
Some image of the Deity,
　Some trace of Him.

'And how can we, then, any scorn
　As foul and dark,
That bear, though frail and lowly, still
　That holy mark ?

And since His impress is upon
　All nature seen,
How can we aught disdain as common
　Or unclean ?

Interior.

"EYES THAT SEE NOT."

ELLA JEWETT.

THEY tell us in the land of song,
Where stately tower and palace rise,
Though marbles breathe and canvas glows,
Though tall cathedrals kiss the skies,
 The peasant, without thought or care,
 Walks on, nor heeds the beauty rare.

We murmur, "Oh, how blind is he !
How destitute of mind and heart !
'Twere worth a fortune *once* to view
Italia's treasured gems of art !"
 Behold the landscape at our feet ! ·
 Was ever painting more complete ?

No need to search for noble souls,
Boccaccio's tale, or Petrarch's song;
A hundred heroes in our midst
Have learned to suffer and be strong,—
 Martyrs whose names will ne'er be known,
 Princes without a crown and throne.

Ah, blind and dull ! Let us not chide
The dwellers in far Italy,
But rather draw the veil aside
From our own eyes, that we may see,
 Lo ! all that seemed but commonplace,
 Adorned with beauty and with grace !

LAMENTATION OF THE LUNGS.

ALAS ! has winter come again ? Oh, how we dread the day !
The sufferings we undergo the bravest might dismay.
It is not that we fear the cold: had we a good supply
Of proper nourishment, the blasts of Greenland we'd defy;
But these poor bodies where we dwell have so impatient grown
That, heedless of the common good, they've learned to slight
 their own.

Not thinking that with fuel we our office would perform,
And take in oxygen to keep the blood and all the body warm.
So *down* the window-sashes go and *up* the *stoves*, until
We starving lungs must labor hard our duty to fulfill.
Perhaps our tabernacle moves to pitch its roving tent
Within some crowded hall or church—no doubt with good in-
    tent;
But little good the sweetest songs or best of sermons do
To those who vainly strive to keep awake within their pew.
For in that place of peace a deadly conflict we must wage,
And friends sit calmly while their lungs in fiercest war engage.
We struggle for a little air, while clamoring for more
The surging flood each moment rolls like waves upon the shore.
Clogged by impurities, in vain to us for help it cries,
And then the brain and nerves grow dull, and dim the droop-
    ing eyes.
But should a sufferer chance to rise and from the topmost raft
Let in a little air, forthwith somebody *feels a draught.*
And so we're forced to get along the very best we can;
Nor do the good that we might do for blundering, headstrong
    man.

                  Phrenological Journal.

———◆———

To READ the English language well, to write with dis-
patch a neat, legible hand, and be master of the first
rules of arithmetic, so as to dispose of at once, with ac-
curacy, every question of figures which comes up in
practice—I call this a good education. And if you add
the ability to write pure grammatical English, I regard it
as an excellent education. These are the tools. You
can do much with them, but you are helpless without
them. They are the foundation; and unless you begin
with these, all your flashy attainments, a little geology,
and all other ologies and osophies are ostentatious rub-
bish.—EDWARD EVERETT.

THE LIGHT-HOUSE.

HIGH o'er the black-backed Skerries, and far
   To the westward hills and the eastward sea,
I shift my light like a twinkling star,
   With ever a star's sweet constancy.
They wait for me when the night comes down,
   And the slow sun falls in his death divine,
Then braving the black night's gathering frown,
   With ruby and diamond blaze—I shine!

There is war at my feet where the black rocks break,
   The thunderous snows of the rising sea;
There is peace above when the stars are awake,
   Keeping their night-long watch with me.
I care not a jot for the roar of the surge,
   The wrath is the sea's—the victory mine!
As over its breadth to the furthest verge,
   Unwavering and untired—I shine!

First on my brow comes the pearly light,
   Dimming my lamp in the new-born day,   ·
One long, last look to left and right,
   And I rest from my toil—for the broad sea-way
Grows bright with the smile and blush of the sky,
   All incandescent and opaline.
I rest—but the loveliest day will die—
   Again in its last wan shadows—I shine!

When the night is black, and the wind is loud,
   And danger is hidden, and peril abroad,
The seaman leaps on the swaying shroud;
   His eye is on me, and his hope in God!
Alone, in the darkness, my blood-red eye
   Meets his, and he hauls his groping line.
" A point to nor'ard !" I hear him cry;
   He goes with a blessing, and still—I shine!

While standing alone in the summer sun
  Sometimes I have visions and dreams of my own,
Of long-life voyages just begun,
  And rocks unnoticed, and shoals unknown;
And I would that men and women would mark
  The duty done by this lamp of mine;
For many a life is lost in the dark,
  And few on earth are the lights that shine !

Good Words.

A SWEDISH POEM.

IT matters little where I was born,
  If my parents were rich or poor;
Whether they shrank at the cold world's scorn,
  Or walked in the pride of wealth secure;
But whether I live an honest man,
  And hold my integrity firm in my clutch,
I tell you, my brother, as plain as I am,
      It matters much!

It matters little how long I stay
  In a world of sorrow and care;
Whether in youth I'm called away,
  Or live till my bones and pate are bare;
But whether I do the best I can
  To soften the weight of adversity's touch
On the faded cheek of my fellow-man,
      It matters much!

It matters little where is my grave,
  On the land or on the sea;
By purling brook or 'neath stormy wave,
  It matters little or naught to me;
But whether the angel Death comes down,
  And marks my brow with his loving touch
As one that shall wear the victor's crown,
      It matters much!

THE DEMON ON THE ROOF.

JOSEPHINE POLLARD.

'TWAS an ancient legend they used to tell
    Within the glow of the kitchen hearth,
When a sudden silence upon them fell,
    And quenched the laughter and noisy mirth:
That whenever a dwelling was building new,
    There were demons ready to curse or bless
The noble structure, that daily grew
    Perfect in shape and comeliness.

And when the sound of the tools had ceased,
    Hammer and nails, and plane and saw,
Ere yet the dwelling could be released
    From the evil spirits,—there was a law
No master-mechanic could be found
    Able or willing to disobey—
That a ladder be left upon the ground
    For their enjoyment, a night and a day.

And when the chimneys begin to roar,
    And voices harsh as the wintry wind
Howl and mock at the outer door,
    The ancient legend is brought to mind,
And we think, perhaps, that a careless loon,
    Not fearing the master's stern reproof,
Has taken the ladder away too soon
    And left a demon upon the roof.

And in every dwelling where joy comes not,
    And the buds of promise forget to bloom,
Be it a palace or be it a cot,
    Amply splendid or scant of room,
We may be sure that a demon elf,
    Fiendishly cruel and full of spite,
Is sitting and grinning away to himself
    Up on the ridge-pole, out of sight.

But let it ever be borne in mind
  By those who often this legend quote,
That with every evil some good we find,
  For every ill there's an antidote.
And if we use but the magic spell,
  And hearts draw near that were kept aloof,
Good angels then in our homes will dwell,
  Despite the demon upon the roof.

ONLY A LITTLE.

DORA GOODALE.

A BIRD has little—only a feather
  Plucked, it may be, from a tender breast,
Only a thread to bind together
  The delicate fabric of his nest;
Yet he sings, '' The wide, free air is mine,
  The dews of earth, the clouds of heaven!''
He sits and swings with the swinging vine,
  And all he looks on to him is given.

A child has little—only a blossom
  Caught at random from fields of bloom.
Only the love in a tender bosom,
  Freed from the shadow of care and gloom;
Yet he laughs all day from the deeps of lightness,
  And feels his joy in the joy of heaven,
He loses himself in a world of brightness,
  And all he asks for to him is given.

A man has little—only a longing
  Higher than labors of sword or pen,
Only a vision whose lights are thronging
  Over the tumult and toil of men.
Yet wealth is his from the wealth of being,
  His are the glories of Earth and Heaven,
He feels a beauty too deep for seeing,
  And all he dreams of to him is given.

4

MY PORTION.

CARLOTTA PERRY.

VERY little good have I,
Wealth and station have passed me by;
But something sweet in my life I hold
That I would not exchange for place or gold.
Beneath my feet the green earth lies,
Above my head are the tender skies;
I look between two heavens; my eyes
Look out to where, serene and sweet,
At the world's fair rim the two heavens meet.

I hear the whispering of the breeze,
The sweet, small tumults amid the trees;
And many a message comes to me
On the wing of bird, in the hum of bee,
From the mountain peak and the surging sea.
E'en the silence speaks a voice so clear,
I lean my very heart to hear,
And all above me and all around
Light and darkness and sight and sound,
To soul and sense such meanings bring,
I thrill with a rapturous wondering.
And I know by many a subtle sign
That the very best of life is mine;
And yet, as I spell each message o'er,
I look and long for a deeper lore;
I long to see and I long to hear,
With a clearer vision, a truer ear;
And I pray with keenest of all desire
For lips that are touched by the altar fire.
Patience, O soul! From a little field
There cometh often a gracious yield;
Who touches His garment's hem is healed.

SAXON GRIT.

REV. ROBERT COLLYER.

WORN by the battle, by Stamford town,
  Fighting the Norman by Hastings bay;
Harold, the Saxon's sun, went down
  When the acorns were falling one autumn day.
Then the Norman said: "I am lord of the land,
  By tenure of conquest here I sit;
I will rule you now with the iron hand;"
  But he had not thought of the Saxon grit.

He took the land, and he took the men,
  And burnt the homesteads from Trent to Tyne;
Made the freemen serfs by a stroke of the pen;
  Ate up the corn and drank the wine.
From the Saxon heart rose a mighty roar,
  Our life shall not be by the king's permit,—
We will fight for the right ; we want no more.
  Then the Norman found out the Saxon grit.

For slow and sure as the oaks had grown
  From the acorns falling that autumn day,
So the Saxon manhood in thorpe and town
  To a nobler nature grew alway.
Winning by inches, holding by clinches,
  Standing by law and the human right;
Many times failing, never once quailing,
  So the new day came out of the night.

Then rising afar in the western sea
  A new world stood in the morn of the day,
Ready to welcome the brave and free,
  Who would wrench out the heart, and march away
From the narrow, contracted, dear old land,
  Where the poor are held by a cruel bit,
To ampler spaces for heart and hand;
  And here was a chance for the Saxon grit.

Steadily steering, eagerly peering,
  Trusting in God, your fathers came,
Pilgrims and strangers, fronting all dangers,
  Cool-headed Saxons, with hearts aflame,
Bound by the letter, but free from the fetter,
  And hiding their freedom in holy writ,
They gave Deuteronomy hints in economy,
  And made a new Moses of Saxon grit,

They whittled and waded through forest and fen,
  Fearless as ever of what might befall,
Pouring out life for the nurture of men
  In the faith that by manhood the world views all.
Inventing baked beans and no end of machines,
  Great with the rifle, and great with the ax,
Sending their notions over the oceans
  To fill empty stomachs and straighten bent backs;

Swift to take chances that end in the dollar,
  Yet open of hand when the dollar is made;
Maintaining the meeting, exalting the scholar,
  But a little too anxious about a good trade.
This is young Jonathan, son of old John,
  Positive, peaceable, firm in the right.
Saxon men all of us, may we be one,
  Steady for freedom and strong in her might.

Then slow and sure, as the oaks have grown
  From the acorns that fell on the dim old day,
So this new manhood, in city and town,
  To a nobler stature will grow alway.
Winning by inches, holding by clinches,
  Slow to contention and slower to quit,
Now and then failing, but never once quailing,
  Let us thank God for the Saxon grit.

THE LITTLE LIGHT.

THE light shone dim on the headland,
    For the storm was raging high;
I shaded my eyes from the inner glare,
    And gazed on the wet, gray sky.
It was dark and lowering; on the sea
    The waves were booming loud,
And the snow and the piercing winter sleet
    Wove over all a shroud.

" God pity the men on the sea to-night !"
    I said to my little ones,
And we shuddered as we heard afar
    The sound of the minute-guns.
My good man came in, in his fishing-coat
    (He was wet and cold that night),
And he said, '' There'll lots of ships go down
    On the headland rocks to-night."

" Let the lamp burn all night, mother,"
    Cried little Mary then;
" Tis but a little light, but still
    It might save drowning men."
" Oh, nonsense !" cried her father
    (He was tired and cross that night),
" The Highland light-house is enough,"
    And he put out the light.

That night, on the rocks below us,
    A noble ship went down;
But one was saved from the ghastly wreck,
    The rest were left to drown.
" We steered by a little light," he said,
    " Till we saw it sink from view:
If they'd only left that light all night,
    My mates might be here, too !"

Then little Mary sobbed aloud,
　　Her father blushed for shame,
" 'Twas our light that you saw," he said,
　　" And I'm the one to blame."
'Twas a little light—how small a thing !
　　And trifling was its cost;
Yet, for want of it a ship went down,
　　And a hundred souls were lost.

WIND AND SEA.

BAYARD TAYLOR.

THE sea is a jovial comrade,
　　He laughs wherever he goes;
His merriment shines in the dimpling lines
　　That wrinkle his hale repose;
He lays himself down at the feet of the sun,
　　And shakes all over with glee;
And the broad-backed billows fall faint on the shore
　　In the mirth of the mighty sea.

But the wind is sad and restless,
　　And cursed with an inward pain;
You may hark as you will by valley or hill,
　　But you hear him still complain.
He wails on the barren mountains,
　　And shrieks on the watery sea;
He sobs in the cedar and moans in the pine,
　　And quakes through the aspen tree.

Welcome are both their voices;
　　And I know not which is best,
The laughter that slips from ocean's lips,
　　Or the comfortless wind's unrest.
There's a pang in all rejoicing,
　　A joy in the heart of pain;
And the wind that saddens, the sea that gladdens,
　　Are singing the self-same strain.

HAPPINESS.

MAGGIE B. PEEKE.

I FOLLOWED a bird to the north and south,·
    I followed it east and west,
With the longing to call it at last my own,
    And hide it within my breast:
But the bird flew on, and I sought in vain,
Through sunshine and wind, through the storm and rain.

I went to the city, to find it, where
    The restless crowd surged by;
But the bird I sought, with its snowy wings
    Had flown to the upper sky,—
And the crowds surged on, with their ceaseless din,
Their waves of sorrow and folly and sin.

I went to the forest, where all day long
    A hush that was sweet fell down,
And I watched for my bird with its magical song,
    But the shadows gave only a frown;
So I knew that I never should find it there,
And I gave up the chase in sullen despair.

I entered the lists of the busy world:
    I took up its burden of care,
Its wrongs to be righted, its sorrows to lift,
    Its mountains of trouble to bear;
And wearied, I laid me at last to rest.
I awoke,—and the bird was within my breast.

AN ILLUMINED TEXT.

THE gray monk, rising, with a loving pride
Laid the long task of patient months aside,
The simple story of the gospels told
In lettering of crimson and of gold;
On its rich pages streamed the setting sun,
And now his life waned and his work was done.

He pushed away the heavy oaken door,
And stood within the sunset calm once more.
Above the narrowing round of life he knew
A sense of beauty and of wonder grew.
The text his art had copied, "God is Love,"
Came to him like the home-returning dove.

As the wind whistled in the bearded grain;
The tender words made music in his brain;
The green leaves whispered of it, everywhere
He read it on the blue scroll of the air,
As if more clearly and in fairer guise
The Lord Himself inscribed it for men's eyes !

Christian at Work.

OLDER than all preached gospels was this unpreached, inarticulate, but ineradicable, for-ever-enduring gospel: work, and therein have well-being. Man, Son of Earth and of Heaven, lies there not, in the innermost heart of thee, a spirit of active method, a force for work ;—and burns like a painfully smouldering fire, giving thee no rest till thou unfold it, till thou write it down in beneficent facts around thee ? What is immethodic, waste, thou shalt make methodic, regulated, arable, obedient and productive to thee. Wheresoever thou findest disorder, there is thy eternal enemy : attack him swiftly, subdue him ; make order of him, the subject not of chaos, but of intelligence, divinity, and thee ! The thistle that grows in thy path, dig it out that a blade of useful grass, a drop of nourishing milk, may grow there instead. The waste cotton-shrub, gather its waste white down, spin it, weave it ; that, in place of idle litter, there may be folded webs, and the naked skin of man be covered.—THOMAS CARLYLE.

THE KING'S BELL.

EBEN E. REXFORD.

" No perfect day has ever come to me,"
    An old man said;
" A perfect day for us can never be
    Till we are dead."

The young king heard him, and he turned away
    In earnest thought.
Did men ne'er find on earth the perfect day
    For which they sought ?

A day all free from care ?—so running o'er
    With life's delight
That there seemed room or wish for nothing more
    From dawn to night ?

" It *must* be that such days have come to man,"
    The young king said.
" Go search—find one who found them—if you can!"
    Ah, wise gray head!

" I trust that some time such a day will come
    To even me,"
The king said. But the old man's lips were dumb—
    A doubter he.

" That you, and those about you all may know
    My perfect day,
A bell shall ring out when the sun is low,
    And men shall say—

" ' Behold! this day has been unto the king
    A day replete
With happiness. It lacked not anything—
    A day most sweet! ' "

In a high tower, ere night, the passers saw
    A mighty bell,
The tidings of a day without a flaw
    Some time to tell.

The bell hung silent in its lofty tower,
    Days came and went;
Each summer brought its sunshine and its flower,
    Its old content;

But not the happy day he hoped to see.
    " But soon or late
The day of days," he said, " will come to me.
    I trust—and wait."

The years, like leaves upon a restless stream,
    Were swept away,
And in the king's dark hair began to gleam
    Bright threads of gray.

Men, passing by, looked upward to the bell,
    And smiling said,
" Delay not of the happy time to tell
    Till we are dead."

But they grew old and died.   And silent still
    The great bell hung;
And the good king, bowed down with age, fell ill
    His cares among.

At dusk, one day, with dazed brain, from his room
    He slowly crept
Up rattling tower-steps, in dust and gloom,
    While watchers slept.

Above the city broke the great bell's voice,
    Silent so long.
" Behold the king's most happy day!   Rejoice!"
    It told the throng.

Filled with strange awe, the long night passed away.
    At morn men said,
" At last the king has found his happy day—
    The king is dead! "

NOBLESSE OBLIGE.

CARLOTTA PERRY.

IF I am weak and you are strong,
    Why then, why then,
To you the braver deeds belong;
    And so, again,
If you have gifts and I have none,
If I have shade and you have sun,
'Tis yours with freer hand to give,
'Tis yours with truer grace to live,
Than I, who giftless, sunless, stand,
With barren life and hand.

We do not ask the little brook
    To turn the wheel;
Unto the larger stream we look.
    The strength of steel
We do not ask from silken bands,
Nor heart of oak in willow wands;
We do not ask the wren to go
Up to the heights the eagles know;
Nor yet expect the lark's clear note
From out the dove's dumb throat.

'Tis wisdom's law, the perfect code,
    By love inspired;
Of him on whom much is bestowed
    Is much required.
The tuneful throat is bid to sing,
The oak must reign the forest's king;
The rushing stream the wheel must move,
The beaten steel its strength must prove.
'Tis given unto the eagle's eyes
To face the midday skies.

USES OF ADVERSITY.

IF none were sick and none were sad,
　What service could we render ?
I think if we were always glad,
　We scarcely could be tender.

Did our beloved never need
　Our patient ministration,
Earth would grow cold, and miss, indeed,
　Its sweetest consolation.

If sorrow never claimed our heart,
　And every wish were granted,
Patience would die and hope depart,
　Life would be disenchanted.

THE VALUE OF LITERATURE.

THE literature of the world is in a very deep sense the direct and most beautiful outcome of its life.　Men have had but a partial success in shaping their external life, but their ideals, their aspirations, their highest thoughts of themselves are to be found in books.　It is only as we unite the actual which we find in its history with the ideal which we find in its literature, that we are able to get any true understanding of an age.　The value and vitality of great books lie not so much in their art as in the fidelity and completeness with which they represent human life.　Literature is, in a word, the best that has been thought or dreamed in the world, and must therefore remain to the very end of time the most fascinating and the most fruitful study to which men can give themselves.—HAMILTON W. MABIE.

TRUE HEROISM.

LET others write of battles fought
  On bloody, ghastly fields,
Where honors greet the man who wins,
  And death the man who yields;
But I will write of him who fights
  And vanquishes his sins,
Who struggles on through weary years
  Against himself and wins.

He is a hero, stanch and brave,
  Who fights an unseen foe,
And puts at last beneath his feet
  His passions base and low;
Who stands erect in manhood's might
  Undaunted, undismayed—
The bravest man that drew a sword
  In foray or in raid.

It calls for something more than brawn
  Or muscle, to overcome
An enemy who marcheth not
  With banner, plume, and drum—
A foe, forever lurking nigh,
  With silent, stealthy tread,
Forever near your board by day,
  And night beside your bed.

All honor, then, to that brave heart,
  Though poor or rich he be,
Who struggles with his baser part—
  Who conquers and is free !
He may not wear a hero's crown,
  Nor fill a hero's grave;
But truth will place his name among
  The bravest of the brave.

The Burial of the Old Flag.

Mary A. Barr.

There is not in all the north countrie,
　　Nor yet on the Humber line,
A town with a prouder record than
　　Newcastle-upon-the-Tyne.
Roman eagles have kept its walls;
　　Saxon, and Dane, and Scot
Have left the glamour of noble deeds,
　　With their names, on this fair spot.
From the reign of William Rufus,
　　The monarchs of every line
Had a grace for loyal Newcastle,
　　The city upon the Tyne.

By the Nuns' Gate, and up Pilgrim Street,
　　What pageants have held their way!
But in seventeen hundred and sixty-three,
　　One lovely morn in May,
There was a sight in bonnie Newcastle!
　　Oh, that I had been there!
To hear the call of the trumpeters
　　Thrilling the clear spring air,
To hear the roar of the cannon,
　　And the drummer's gathering beat,
And the eager hum of the multitudes
　　Waiting upon the street.

Just at noon was a tender hush,
　　And a funeral march was heard;
With arms reversed and colors tied
　　Came the men of the Twenty-third.
And Lennox, their noble leader, bore
　　The shreds of a faded flag,
The battle-flag of the regiment,
　　Shot to a glorious rag;

Shot into shreds upon its staff,
  Torn in a hundred fights,
From the torrid plains of India
  To the cold Canadian heights.

There was not an inch of bunting left;
  How could it float again
Over the faithful regiment
  It never had led in vain?
And oh, the hands that had carried it!
  It was not cloth and wood:
It stood for a century's heroes,
  And was crimson with their blood;
It stood for a century's comrades.
  They could not cast it away,
And so with a soldier's honors
  They were burying it that day.

In the famous old North Humber fort,
  Where the Roman legions trod,
With the roar of cannon and roll of drums
  They laid it under the sod.
But it wasn't a tattered flag alone
  They buried with tender pride;
It was every faithful companion
  That under the flag had died.
It was honor, courage, and loyalty
  That thrilled that mighty throng
Standing bare-headed and silent as
  The old flag passed along.

So when the grasses had covered it
  There was a joyful strain;
And the soldiers, stirred to a noble thought,
  Marched proudly home again.
The citizens went to their shops once more,
  The collier went to his mine;
The shepherd went to the broomy hills,
  And the sailor to the Tyne;

But men and women and children felt
  That it had been well to be
Just for an hour or two face to face
  With honor and loyalty.

THE OLD STONE BASIN.

SUSAN COOLIDGE.

IN the heart of the busy city,
  In the scorching noontide heat,
A sound of bubbling water
  Falls on the din of the street.

It falls in a gray stone basin,
  And over the cool wet brink
The heads of thirsty horses
  Each moment are stretched to drink.

And peeping between the crowding heads
  As the horses come and go,
"The Gift of Three Little Sisters"
  Is read on the stone below.

Ah, beasts are not taught letters,
  They know no alphabet;
And never a horse in all these years
  Has read the words; and yet

I think that each toil-worn creature
  Who stops to drink by the way,
His thanks in his own dumb fashion
  To the sisters small must pay.

Years have gone by since busy hands
  Wrought at the basin's stone;
The kindly little sisters
  Are all to women grown.

I do not know their home or fates,
   Or the name they bear to men,
But this sweetness of their gracious deed
   Is just as fresh as then.

And all life long, and after life,
   They must the happier be,
For the cup of water given by them
   When they were children three.

————◆————

BESIDE THE RAILWAY TRACK.

ON its straight iron pathway the long train was rushing,
   With its noise, and its smoke, and its great human load;
And I saw a wild rose that in beauty was blushing,
   Fresh and sweet, by the side of the hot, dusty road.

Untrained were its branches, untended it flourished,
   No eye watched its opening or mourned its decay;
But its leaves by the soft dews of heaven were nourished,
   And it opened its buds in the warm light of day.

I asked why it grew there where none prized its beauty,
   For of thousands who passed none had leisure to stay.
And the answer came sweetly, " I do but my duty;
   I was told to grow here by the side of the way."

There are those on life's pathway whose spirits are willing
   To dwell where the busy crowd passes them by;
But the dew from above on their leaves is distilling,
   And they bloom 'neath the smile of the All-seeing Eye.

They are loved by the few—like the rose, they remind us,
   When tempted from duty's safe pathway to stray;
We, too, have a place and a mission assign'd us,
   Though it be but to grow by the side of the way.

5

A Song for the Conquered.

William W. Story.

I sing the Hymn of the Conquered, who fell in the battle of
  life;
The hymn of the wounded, the beaten, who died overwhelmed
  in the strife.
Not the jubilant song of the victors, for whom the resounding
  acclaim
Of nations was lifted in chorus, whose brows wore the chaplet
  of fame.
But the hymn of the low and the humble, the weary, the
  broken in heart,
Who strove and who failed, acting bravely a silent and desperate part;
Whose youth bore no flower in its branches, whose hopes
  burned in ashes away;
From whose hands slipped the prize they had grasped at; who
  stood at the dying of day
With the work of their life all around them, unpitied, un-
  heeded, alone,
With death swooping down o'er their failure, and all but their
  faith overthrown.

While the voice of the world shouts its chorus,—its pæan for
  those who have won,—
While the trumpet is sounding triumphant, and high to the
  breeze and the sun
Gay banners are waving, hands clapping, and hurrying feet
Thronging after the laurel-crowned victors, I stand on the
  field of defeat,
In the shadow 'mongst those who are fallen, and wounded and
  dying, and there
Chant a requiem low, place my hand on their pain-knotted
  brows, breathe a prayer,

Hold the hand that is hapless, and whisper, "They only the
    victory win
Who have fought the good fight, and have vanquished the
    demon that tempts us within;
Who have held to their faith unseduced by the prize that the
    world holds on high;
Who have dared for a high cause to suffer, resist, fight—if
    need be to die."

Speak, History! Who are life's victors? Unroll thy long
    annals, and say—
Are they those whom the world called the victors who won the
    success of the day?
The martyrs, or Nero? The Spartans who fell at Thermopylæ's
    tryst,
Or the Persians of Xerxes? His judges, or Socrates? Pilate,
    or Christ?

THE AMEN OF THE ROCKS.

CHRISTIAN GELLERT.

THE Venerable Bede, with age grown blind,
    Still went abroad to preach the new evangel.
From town to town, village to village, journeyed
    The saintly elder, with a lad for guide,
And preached the word with youthful zeal and fervor;
    And once the lad led him along a vale,
All scattered o'er with mighty moss-grown bowlders.

More thoughtless than malicious quoth the urchin,
    " Here, reverend father, many men have come,
And all the multitude await thy sermon."
    The blind old man stood upright at his speech,
    And spake his text, explained it, thence digressed,
    Exhorted, warned, reproved, and comforted,
    So earnestly that tears of love and joy
    Ran down his cheeks, and on his long gray beard;

Then, as was meet, he ended with "Our Father,
    Thine is the kingdom, Thine the power, and Thine
The glory is forever and forever."
Then came a thousand, thousand answering voices—
"Yea, reverend father, amen and amen."
Then, terrified, the boy fell down repentant,
    Confessing to the saint his ill behavior.

"Son," said the holy man, "didst thou read never
That stones themselves shall cry if man is silent?
    Play thou no more, my son, with things divine.
    God's word is powerful, and cuts more sharp
    Than any two-edged sword. And if it be
That man toward the Lord is stony-hearted,
A human heart shall wake in stones, and witness."

ONLY A LITTLE THING.

MRS. M. P. HANDY.

IT was only a tiny seed,
    Carelessly brushed aside;
But it grew in time to a noxious weed,
    And spread its poison wide.

It was only a little leak,
    So small you might hardly see;
But the rising waters found the break,
    And wrecked the great levee.

It was only a single spark,
    Dropped by a passing train;
But the dead leaves caught, and swift and dark
    Was its work on wood and plain.

It was only an unsound nail
    That the workman used—ah me!
But the ship that else had weathered the gale
    Went down in the deep, dark sea.

It was only a thoughtless word,
   Scarce meant to be unkind;
But it pierced as a dart to the heart that heard,
   And left its sting behind.

It may seem a trifle at most,
   The thing that we do or say;
And yet it may be that at fearful cost
   We may wish it undone some day.

THE LITTLE MESSENGER OF LOVE.

'TWAS a little sermon preached to me
   By a sweet, unconscious child—
A baby girl, scarce four years old,
   With blue eyes soft and mild.
It happened on a rainy day;
   I, seated in a car,
Was thinking, as I neared my home,
   Of the continual jar
And discord that pervade the air
   Of busy city life,
Each caring but for "number one,"
   Self-gain provoking strife.
The gloomy weather seemed to cast
   On every face a shade,
But on one countenance were lines
   By sorrow deeply laid.
With low bowed head and hands clasped close,
   She sat, so poor and old,
Nor seemed to heed the scornful glance
   From eyes unkind and cold.
I looked again. Oh, sweet indeed
   The sight that met my eyes!
Sitting upon her mother's lap,
   With baby face so wise,
Was a wee child with sunny curls,

Blue eyes, and dimpled chin,
And a young, pure, loving heart
　　Unstained as yet by sin.
Upon the woman poor and sad
　　Her eyes in wonder fell,
Till wonder changed to pitying love;
　　Her thoughts, oh, who could tell?
Her tiny hands four roses held;
　　She looked them o'er and o'er,
Then choosing out the largest one,
　　She struggled to the floor.
Across the swaying car she went
　　Straight to the woman's side,
And putting in the wrinkled hand
　　The rose, she ran to hide
Her little face in mother's lap,
　　Fearing she had done wrong,
Not knowing, baby as she was,
　　That she had helped along
The up-hill road of life a soul
　　Cast down, discouraged quite,
As on the woman's face there broke
　　A flood of joyous light.

Dear little child ! she was indeed
　　A messenger of love
Sent to that woman's lonely heart
　　From the great Heart above.
This world would be a different place
　　Were each to give to those
Whose hearts are sad as much of love
　　As went with baby's rose.

Harper's Young People.

I'D RATHER be right than to be President of the United
States.—HENRY CLAY.

ORIGINAL MAXIMS OF GEORGE WASHINGTON.

[Recitations for Twelve Students.]

I.

COMMERCE and industry are the best mines of a nation.

II.

Let your heart feel for the afflictions and distresses of every one.

III.

Ingratitude, I hope, will never constitute a part of my character, nor find a place in my bosom.

IV.

Labor to keep alive in your breast that little spark of celestial fire called conscience.

V.

To persevere is one's duty, and to be silent is the best answer to calumny.

VI.

I never wish to promise more than I have a moral certainty of performing.

VII.

I shall never attempt to palliate my own foibles by exposing the error of another.

VIII.

It is a maxim with me not to ask what, under similar circumstances, I would not grant.

IX.

Be courteous to all, but intimate with few ; and let those be well tried before you give them your confidence.

X.

Associate with men of good quality if you esteem your own reputation, for it is better to be alone than in bad company.

XI.

A good character is the first essential in a man. It is, therefore, highly important to endeavor not only to be learned, but virtuous.

XII.

I am resolved that no misrepresentations, falsehoods, or calumny shall make me swerve from what I conceive to be the strict line of duty.

THE WORK OF A SUNBEAM.

NATHAN G. SHEPHERD.

I HAVE read in old tales of the buried past,
    Of two armies which met on the battle-plain;
Roman and Cymbric, in numbers vast,
    How they fought till the field was heaped with slain;
And how through all day the crimson tide
    Of battle favored the Cymbric side,
        Though their dead bestrewed the plain,

Till at length, from out of the clouded skies,
    A sunbeam darted across the world,
Blinding the Cymbrian warrior's eyes;
    And backward their conquering hosts were hurled.
And thus in the record of years is told
How a sunbeam, back in the days of old,
        Decided the fate of the world.

THE SILVER BIRD'S NEST.

A STRANDED soldier's epaulet
　　The waters cast ashore,
A little wingèd rover met,
　　And eyed it o'er and o'er;
The silver bright so charmed her sight,
　　On that lone idle vest,
She knew not why she should deny
　　Herself a silver nest.

The shining wire she pecked and twirled,
　　Then bore it to her bough,
Where on a flowery twig 'twas curled,
　　The bird can show you how;
But when enough of that bright stuff
　　The cunning builder bore,
Her house to make, she would not take,
　　Nor did she covet, more.

And when the little artisan—
　　While neither pride nor guilt
Had entered in her pretty plan—
　　Her resting-place had built,
With here and there a plume to spare,
　　About her own light form,
Of these, inlaid with skill, she made
　　A lining soft and warm.

But do you think the tender brood
　　She fondled there, and fed,
Were prouder when they understood
　　The sheen about their bed ?
Do you suppose they ever rose,
　　Of higher powers possessed,
Because they knew they peeped and grew
　　Within a silver nest ?

LUTHER.

JOAQUIN MILLER.

VALIANT, defiant, and free,
  Majestic, impressive, and lone,
He looms like that isle of the sea
  That rose to an emperor's throne.

Honor where manhood is found,
  Glory where valor has led,
To priest or not priest, the world round;
  To white man, or black man, or red.

Honor to manhood and worth,
  Glory to action and deed,
To manhood, not priesthood, on earth;
  For man is the master of creed.

ORIGINAL MAXIMS OF JAMES A. GARFIELD.

[Recitations for Ten Students.]

I.

A POUND of pluck is worth a ton of luck.

II.

Poets may be born, but success is made.

III.

Be fit for more than the one thing you are now doing.

IV.

I would rather be beaten in right than succeed in
wrong.

V.

Luck is an *ignis fatuus.* You may follow it to ruin,
but not to success.

VI.

If the power to do hard work is not a talent, it is the best possible substitute for it.

VII.

I would rather be defeated than make capital out of my religion.

VIII.

Things don't turn up in this world unless somebody turns them up.

IX.

Territory is but the body of a nation. The people who inhabit its hills and its valleys are its soil, its spirit, and its life.

X.

The privilege of being a young man is a great privilege, and the privilege of growing to be an independent man, in middle life, is a greater.

IT IS a strange fancy of mine, but I cannot help wishing we could move for returns—as their phrase is in parliament—for the suffering caused in any one day, or other period of time, throughout the world, to be arranged under certain heads ; and we should then see what the world has occasion to fear most. What a large amount would come under the heads of unreasonable fear of others, of miserable quarrels amongst relations upon infinitesimally small subjects, of imaginary slights, of undue cares, of false shames, of absolute misunderstandings, of unnecessary pains to maintain credit or reputation, of vexation that we cannot make others of the same mind with ourselves ! What a wonderful thing it would be to see set down in figures, as it were, how ingenious we are in plaguing one another !—ARTHUR HELPS.

THE ANGEL OF DAWN.

J. S. CUTLER.

ONE morn an angel stopped beside my door,
  Clad in the shining garments of the dawn;
Upon his brow a starry crown he wore;
  In his right hand a flaming sword was drawn.
With terror filled, I prayed with piteous cry
The angel-presence then to pass me by.

" I am not death," the angel said, and smiled;
  " Thy soul shall have the answer to thy prayer.
Drive from thy breast this fearful anguish wild;
  I am the Angel of the Dawn—beware !
I place a priceless jewel in thy hands;
The day is thine, waste not its running sands.

" Therefore mark well—thy duty waiteth thee,
  Beside the morning's swiftly opening gate;
The new day dawns—its hours will quickly flee;
  Stamp them with honor ere it be too late;
Thy deed may lift thee higher than thy prayer.
The day is thine, remember and beware !"

And then the angel took his shining way,
  On silent wings, out to the shadowy west;
And swiftly onward came the new-born day,
  The priceless jewel of my angel-guest.
The birds awoke and filled the world with song,
And made my burden light the whole day long.

And now, when morning throws its early beams
  In golden rays across the ocean's floor,
And I awake from slumbering and dreams,
  I know an angel waiteth at the door;
I hear again that kindly voice declare—
" Thy deed may lift thee higher than thy prayer."

QUESTIONS.

KATE LAWRENCE.

CAN you put the spider's web back in its place that once has
been swept away?

Can you put the apple again on the bough which fell at our
feet to-day?

Can you put the lily-cup back on the stem, and cause it to live
and.grow?

Can you mend the butterfly's broken wing that you crushed
with a hasty blow?

Can you put the bloom again on the grape, or the grape again
on the vine?

Can you put the dew-drops back on the flowers and make them
sparkle and shine?

Can you put the petals back on the rose? If you could, would
it smell as sweet?

Can you put the flour again in the husk, and show me the
ripened wheat?

Can you put the kernel back in the nut, or the broken egg in
its shell?

Can you put the honey back in the comb, and cover with wax
each cell?

Can you put the perfume back in the vase, when once it has
sped away?

Can you put the corn-silk back on the corn, or the down on
catkins—say?

You think that my questions are trifling, then? Let me ask
you another one:

Can a hasty word ever be unsaid, or a deed unkind undone?

THE LANDING OF THE PILGRIMS.

FELICIA HEMANS.

Plymouth (Dec. 21, 1620).

THE breaking waves dashed high
On a stern and rock-bound coast,
And the woods against a stormy sky
Their giant branches tossed;

And the heavy night hung dark
The hills and waters o'er,
When a band of exiles moored their bark,
On the wild New England shore.

What sought they thus afar ?
Bright jewels of the mine ?
The wealth of seas, the spoils of war ?—
They sought a faith's pure shrine !

Ay, call it holy ground,
The soil where first they trod;
They have left unstained what there they found—
Freedom to worship God.

THE TWENTY-FIRST OF FEBRUARY.

WILLIAM CULLEN BRYANT.

PALE is the February sky,
And brief the mid-day's sunny hours;
The wind-swept forest seems to sigh
For the sweet time of leaves and flowers.

Yet has no month a prouder day,
Not even when the summer broods
O'er meadows in their fresh array,
Or autumn tints the glowing woods.

For this chill season now again
  Brings, in its annual round, the morn
When, greatest of the sons of men,
  Our glorious Washington was born.

Lo, where, beneath an icy shield,
  Calmly the mighty Hudson flows !
By snow-clad fell and frozen field,
  Broadening, the lordly river goes.

The wildest storm that sweeps through space,
  And rends the oak with sudden force,
Can raise no ripple on his face,
  Or slacken his majestic course.

Thus, 'mid the wreck of thrones, shall live
  Unmarred, undimmed, our hero's fame,
And years succeeding years shall give
  Increase of honors to his name.

FOREFATHERS' DAY.

HELEN HUNT JACKSON.

FIND me the men on earth who care
  Enough for faith or creed to-day
To seek a barren wilderness
  For simple liberty to pray.

Despise their narrow creed who will;
  Pity their poverty who dare:
Their lives knew joys, their lives wore crowns,
  We do not know, we cannot wear.

And if so be that it is saved,
  Our poor Republic, stained and bruised,
'Twill be because we lay again
  Their corner-stones which we refused.

A True Story.

"Where is the baby, grandmamma?"
　　The sweet young mother calls
From her work in the cosy kitchen,
　　With its dainty whitewashed walls.
And grandma leaves her knitting,
　　And looks for her all around;
But not a trace of baby dear
　　Can anywhere be found.

No sound of its merry prattle,
　　No gleam of its sunny hair,
No patter of tiny footsteps,
　　No sign of it anywhere.
All through house and garden,
　　Far out into the field,
They search each nook and corner;
　　But nothing is revealed.

And the mother's face grew pallid;
　　Grandmamma's eyes grew dim;
The father's gone to the village;
　　No use to look for him.
And the baby lost!　"Where's Rover!"
　　The mother chanced to think
Of the old well in the orchard
　　Where the cattle used to drink.

"Where's Rover?　I know he'd find her?
　　Rover!"　In vain they call,
Then hurry away to the orchard;
　　And there by the moss-grown wall,
Close to the well, lies Rover,
　　Holding to baby's dress;
She was leaning over the wall's edge
　　In perfect fearlessness!

She stretched her little arms down;
But Rover held her fast,
And never seemed to mind the kicks
The tiny bare feet cast
So spitefully upon him,
But wagged his tail instead,
To greet the frightened searchers,
While naughty baby said:

" Dere's a 'ittle dirl in the 'ater;
She's dust as big as me,
Mamma; I want to help her out,
And take her home to tea.
But Rover, he won't let me,
And I don't love him.   Go
Away, you naughty Rover !
Oh ! why are you crying so ?"

The mother kissed her, saying:
" My darling, understand,
Good Rover saved your life, my dear—
And, see, he licks your hand !
Kiss Rover."   Baby struck him,
But grandma understood;
She said: " It's hard to thank the friend
Who thwarts us for our good."

Baldwin's Monthly.

6

LITTLE CHRISTEL.

MRS. MARY E. BRADLEY.

FRÄULEIN, the young schoolmistress, to her pupils said one day,
" Next week, at Pfingster holiday, King Ludwig rides this way;
And you will be wise, my little ones, to work with a will at
    your tasks,
That so you may answer fearlessly whatever question he asks.
It would be a shame too dreadful if the king should have it to
    tell
That Hansel missed in his figures, and Peterkin could not
    spell."

" Oho ! that never shall happen," cried Hansel and Peterkin
    too;
" We'll show King Ludwig, when he comes, what the boys in
    this school can do."
" And we," said Gretchen and Bertha, and all the fair little
    maids
Who stood in a row before her, with their hair in flaxen braids,
" We will pay such good attention to every word you say,
That you shall not be ashamed of us when King Ludwig rides
    this way."

She smiled, the young schoolmistress, to see that they loved
    her so,
And with patient care she taught them the things it was good
    to know.
Day after day she drilled them till the great day came at last,
When the heralds going before him blew out their sounding
    blast;
And with music, and flying banners, and the clatter of horses,
    feet,
The king and his troops of soldiers rode down the village street.

Oh the hearts of the eager children beat fast with joy and fear,
And Fräulein trembled and grew pale as the cavalcade drew
    near;

But she blushed with pride and pleasure when the lessons
    came to be heard,
For in all the flock of the boys and girls not one of them
    missed a word.
And King Ludwig turned to the teacher with a smile and a
    gracious look;
"It is plain," said he, "that your scholars have carefully
    conned their book.

"But now let us ask some questions to see if they understand;"
And he showed to one of the little maids an orange in his hand.
It was Christel, the youngest sister of the mistress fair and
    kind—
A child with a face like a lily, and as lovely and pure a mind.
"What kingdom does this belong to?" as he called her to his
    knee;
And at once—"The vegetable," she answered quietly.

"Good," said the monarch kindly, and showed her a piece of
    gold;
"Now tell me what this belongs to—the pretty coin that I
    hold?"
She touched it with careful finger, for gold was a metal
    rare,
And then—"The mineral kingdom!" she answered with con-
    fident air.
"Well done for the little mädchen!" And good King Ludwig
    smiled
At Fräulein and her sister, the teacher and the child.

"Now answer me one more question,"—with a twinkle of fun
    in his eye:
"What kingdom do I belong to?" For he thought she would
    make reply,
"The animal;" and he meant to ask with a frown if that was
    the thing
For a little child like her to say to her lord and master, the
    king?

He knew not the artless wisdom that would set his wit at
    naught,
And the little Christel guessed nothing at all of what was in
    his thought.

But her glance shot up at the question, and the brightness in
    her face,
Like a sunbeam on a lily, seemed to shine all over the place.
"What kingdom do *you* belong to ?" her innocent lips repeat;
" Why, surely, the kingdom of Heaven !" rings out the answer
    sweet.
And then for a breathless moment a sudden silence fell,
And you might have heard the fall of a leaf as they looked at
    little Christel.

But it only lasted a moment, then rose as sudden a shout—
"Well done, well done for little Christel !" and the bravos
    rang about.
For the king in his arms had caught her, to her wondering,
    shy surprise,
And over and over he kissed her, with a mist of tears in his
    eyes.
"May the blessing of God," he murmured, "forever rest on
    thy head !
Henceforth, by His grace, my life shall prove the truth of what
    thou hast said."

He gave her the yellow orange, and the golden coin for her own,
And the school had a royal feast that day whose like they had
    never known.
To Fräulein, the gentle mistress, he spoke such words of cheer
That they lightened her anxious labor for many and many a
    year.
And because in his heart was hidden the memory of this thing,
The Lord had a better servant, the Lord had a wiser king !

CONCERT RECITATIONS.

SONGS OF THE SEASONS.

META E. B. THORNE.

[*For Four Students.*]

SPRING.

THE king of the day is exerting his power,
  And night and cold at his bidding depart;
All nature in this resurrection hour
  Will welcome my advent with joyous heart.
Then hasten, my children! Ho, March winds wild,
  O'er mountain and valley, blow, madly blow!
Proclaim the glad coming of springtime mild,
  And speed the departure of frost and snow!
Ye clouds of April, drop down your showers,
  And fill to the brim the rivers and rills ﹐
With liquid laughter; May's delicate flowers
  Await your dripping 'mong valleys and hills.

SUMMER.

Spring scattered the seed with a lavish hand,
  Her whispering breezes and magic showers
Awoke into life; see the serried ranks stand
  Of fervid July's lush grasses and flowers.
Then August comes with her sultry noons
  Whose hot breath gildeth the ripening grain,
And the glorious light of her harvest moons;
  Now the reaper sings as he sweeps the plain:
" My gleaming scythe I swing to and fro;
  Before it is falling the golden wheat—
A precious store for the time of the snow;
  All praise to the Giver of mercies so sweet!"

AUTUMN.

The plentiful harvest is garnered in;
  But I bring September's bounteous store
Of glowing fruitage, all hearts to win;
  Now the summer's brilliant reign is o'er.
Now, royal October the scepter wields,
  In whose wealth of rosy and mellow light
Seem glorified even the bare brown fields,
  With their delicate veil of haze bedight.
And e'en when November, dark and chill,
  In her cloud-robe somber broods o'er the earth,
When the birds are hushed 'mid woodland and hill,
  And the flowers are asleep till the spring's glad birth,
There are blossoms still for the trustful heart,
  Sweet hopes for what life may yet unfold,
And memories precious that will not depart
  When fades from the hill-tops the autumn's gold.

WINTER.

I bring to the waiting fields the snow,
  December's mantle so soft and pure,
That covers the sleeping seeds below,
  To remain, till the spring's return, secure.
Ye think my touch unkind and rude
  When the bracing frost and cold I bring,
Ye chant in a pining, reproachful mood
  The praises of summer and dewy spring;
Yet oft at my touch the baleful seeds
  Of pestilence powerless fall in death;
New vigor to youth and prime proceeds
  From my clear, keen, purifying breath.
Bnt richer delights to you I bring;
  For mine is the anniversary time,
When " Good-will to men!" the angels sing,
  " Good-will!" the echoing joy-bells chime.

THE COMING OF SPRING.

WILHELM MÜLLER.

Solo.   UP with windows, up with hearts!
Concert.   Swiftly, swiftly!
Solo.   Graybeard Winter seeks to go,
      He wanders troubled to and fro,
      He beats his breast full fearfully
      And packs his duds right hastily,
Concert.   With speed, with speed.

Solo.   Up with windows, up with hearts!
Concert.   Swiftly, swiftly!
Solo.   The Springtime knocks and stamps without—
      And listen to his joyous shout!—
      Before the door he takes his stand,
      With beauteous flower-buds in his hand,
Concert.   With speed, with speed.

Solo.   Open windows, open hearts!
Concert.   Swiftly, swiftly!
Solo.   The brave young South-wind stands below,
      With round red cheeks and eyes aglow,
      And blows that doors and windows rattle,
      Till Winter yields him in the battle—
Concert.   With speed, with speed.

Concert.   Open windows, open hearts!
      With speed, with speed.!
      Wild birds sound the battle-song—
      And hark, and hark! an echo long,
      An echo from my inmost heart—
      The joys of Spring bid Winter part
      With speed, with speed.

THE GOOD TIME COMING.

CHARLES MACKAY.

Concert. THERE'S a good time coming, boys,
  A good time coming.
Solo. We may not live to see the day,
  But earth shall glisten in the ray
  Of the good time coming.
  Cannon-balls may aid the truth,
   But thought's a weapon stronger;
  We'll win our battle by its aid—
   Wait a little longer.

Concert. There's a good time coming, boys,
  A good time coming.
Solo. The pen shall supersede the sword,
  And Right, not Might, shall be the lord
  In the good time coming.
  Worth, not Birth, shall rule mankind,
   And be acknowledged stronger;
  The proper impulse has been given—
   Wait a little longer.

Concert. There's a good time coming, boys,
  A good time coming.
Solo. War in all men's eyes shall be
  A monster of iniquity
  In the good time coming;
  Nations shall not quarrel then,
   To prove which is the stronger;
  Nor slaughter men for glory's sake—
   Wait a little longer.

Concert. There's a good time coming, boys,
  A good time coming.
Solo. Hateful rivalries of creed
  Shall not make their martyrs bleed

In the good time coming.
Religion shall be shorn of pride,
  And flourish all the stronger;
And Charity shall trim her lamp—
  Wait a little longer.

Concert. There's a good time coming, boys,
    A good time coming.
Solo. Little children shall not toil,
  Under or above the soil,
    In the good time coming;
  But shall play in healthful fields
    Till limb and mind grow stronger;
  And every one shall read and write—
    Wait a little longer.

Concert. There's a good time coming, boys,
    A good time coming.
Solo. The people shall be temperate,
  And shall love instead of hate
    In the good time coming.
  They shall use, and not abuse,
    And make all virtue stronger;
  The reformation has begun—
    Wait a little longer.

Concert. There's a good time coming, boys,
    A good time coming.
  Let us aid it all we can,
  Every woman, every man,
    The good time coming.
  Smallest helps, if rightly given,
    Make the impulse stronger;
  'Twill be strong enough one day—
    Wait a little longer.

THE CHARGE AT WATERLOO.

SIR WALTER SCOTT.

[*For Boy's Recitation.*]

ON came the whirlwind—like the last
But fiercest sweep of tempest blast;
On came the whirlwind—steel-gleams broke
Like lightning through the rolling smoke:
    The war was waked anew.
Three hundred cannon-mouths roared loud,
And from their throats with flash and cloud
    Their showers of iron threw.
In one dark torrent, broad and strong,
The advancing onset rolled along.
But on the British heart were lost
The terrors of the charging host;
For not an eye the storm that viewed
Changed its proud glance of fortitude;
Nor was one forward footstep stayed
As dropped the dying and the dead.
Down were the eagle-banners sent,
Down reeling steeds and riders went;
Corselets were pierced and pennons rent,
    And, to augment the fray,
Wheeled full against their staggering flanks,
The English horsemen's foaming ranks
    Forced their resistless way.
Then to the musket-knell succeeds
The clash of swords, the neigh of steeds;
As plies the smith his clanging trade,
Against the cuirass rang the blade;
And while amid their scattered band
Raged the fierce rider's bloody brand,
Recoiled in common rout and fear
Lancer and guard and cuirassier,
Horsemen and foot—a mingled host—
Their leaders fallen, their standards lost.

SUMMER STORM.

JAMES RUSSELL LOWELL.

[Abbreviated for Concert Recitation.]

[The following selection is peculiarly effective for concert recitation on account of the great number and variety of vocal changes. The italicized words should be given with abrupt, explosive sounds; the italicized final consonants with extreme distinctness of articulation ; the pauses indicated by dashes should be exaggerated, and the time most accurately marked.]

Suddenly—all the sky is hid
  As with the *shutting* of a *lid*.
One—by—one—great—drops—are falling,
  Doubtful—and—slow.
Down the pane they are crookedly crawling,
  And the win*d*—breathes low.

Now—on the hills—I hear the thunder—mutter,
  The win*d*—is gathering in the wes*t*.
The upturned leaves first whiten and flutter
  Then droo*p*—to a fitful res*t*.
Now *leaps* the *wind* on the sleepy marsh,
  And *tramples* the *grass* with *terrified feet.*
The *startled river* turns leaden and harsh,
  You can *hear* the *quick heart* of the tempest *beat.*

Look, look ! that *livid flash !*
And instantly follows the rattling thunder
As if some cloud-crag—split asunder—
Fell—splintering with a ruinous *crash.*
Against the windows, the storm comes *dashing ;*
Through tattered foliage, the hail—tears crashing;
  The blue *lightning—flashes*,
  The *rapid hail clashes*,

The white waves are tumbling,
  And in one baffled roar,
The thunder—is rumbling—
  And crashing and crumbling.

(*Whisper*) { Hush!   Still as death
{ The tempes*t*—holds his breath—
  As from a sudden will.
 The rain—stops—short—but from the eaves
 You see it dro*p* and hear it—on the leaves,
(*Half-whisper*) All—is—so—still.

 Gone—gone—so soon !
 The pale and quiet moon
 Makes her calm forehead bare.
No more my half-crazed fancy there.
Can sha*p*e—a gian*t*—in the air,
And the last fragments of the storm,
Like shattered rigging from a figh*t* at sea,
Silen*t* and few—are drifting over me.

SONG OF THE STEAMER ENGINE.
C. B. LEROW.

[This selection is adapted for Solo and Concert recitation. The first two
and last two lines of each stanza, and *the whole of the last stanza*, are to be
given in concert. The other lines can be assigned to one or to six students—
the latter arrangement giving greater variety, as the stanzas differ widely in
style. As the refrain, or chorus, is to imitate the peculiar beat or rhythm of
the engine, the accent must fall upon the third syllable of each line, while
each syllable is given with *staccato* effect, and the whole line on a monotone.
The fifth stanza represents two equal beats on the two syllables—the rhythm
of the engine when moving in half time on account of danger.]

I.

  " WE are ready for work—
  We are ready for work—"
So says the great engine when we start
And the steam comes up from its pulsing heart.
With its hundred iron arms and hands
It is waiting to take us to foreign lands,
And it says in the cheeriest sort of way
While our friends are watching us down the bay,
  " We are ready for work—
  We are ready for work—"

II.

"We will carry you over—
  We will carry you over—"
It seems to say on the ocean wide
When no land can be seen on either side;
And we wonder how it can ever be
That we can go straight o'er the trackless sea.
And we watch the engine day by day,
Encouraged by what it seems to say,
  "We will carry you over—
  We will carry you over—"

III.

"Our work is praying—
  Our work is praying—"
It says on the sunny Sabbath day
When the passengers meet to sing and pray;
And through the sermon and chanted psalm
We listen with hearts subdued and calm
To the faithful strokes of the engine strong
As over the ocean we sail along;
  "Our work is praying—
  Our work is praying—"

IV.

"Sleep safe till morning—
  Sleep safe till morning—"
Are the words we hear in the dead of night
When only the sailors can see a light;
And the great ship rushes along as free
As if the sunshine were on the sea;
And we rest secure near the beating heart
Of the engine doing its noble part;
  "Sleep safe till morning—
  Sleep safe till morning—"

V.

    " Don't fear—
      Don't fear—"
It can say no more in the heavy fog
Which seems its very breath to clog;
While with hearts grown faint and lips that pray
We think of the friends who are far away,
And of hidden perils and sudden death
Although the engine pants under breath,
    " Don't fear—
      Don't fear—"

VI.

    " It is all right now—
      It is all right now—
Are the words we hear when the sun peeps through
And the leaden clouds catch a tint of blue;
And the iron arms work hard and fast,
For we are in sight of the land at last.
And the engine seems as glad as we
That the ship is now from all danger free.
    " It is all right now—
      It is all right now—"

VII.

O brave engine, you little know
What to your faithful heart we owe.
You did your duty by day and night;
As well in the darkness as the light;
Never letting an hour go by,
Never stopping to question Why—
Showing what beauty and grace can be
In honest Toil and Fidelity.

THE CHILD ON THE JUDGMENT-SEAT.

MRS. E. CHARLES.

[*Recitation for Two Students.*]

FIRST.

WHERE hast thou been toiling all day, sweetheart,
  That thy brow is burdened and sad ?
The Master's work may make weary feet,
  But it leaves the spirit glad.

SECOND.

No pleasant garden-toils were mine;
  I have sat on the judgment-seat
Where the Master sits above, and calls
  The children around His feet.

FIRST.

How camest thou on the judgment-seat ?
  Sweetheart, who set thee there ?
'Tis a lonely and lofty seat for thee,
  And well might fill thee with care.

SECOND.

I climbed on the judgment-seat myself,
  I have sat there alone all day,
For it grieved me to see the children around
  Idling their life away.

FIRST.

And what didst thou on the judgment-seat,
  Sweetheart, what didst thou there ?
Would the idlers heed thy childish voice ?
  Did the garden mend for thy care ?

SECOND.

Nay, that grieved me more; I called and I cried,
  But they left me there forlorn;
My voice was weak, and they heeded not,
  Or they laughed my words to scorn.

FIRST.

Ah, the judgment-seat was not for thee,
  The servants were not thine,
And the eyes which fix the praise and the blame
  See farther than thine or mine.

SECOND.

Should I see the Master's treasures lost,
  The gifts that should feed his poor,
And not lift my voice—be it weak as it may—
  And not be grievèd sore ?

FIRST.

But how fared thy garden-plot, sweetheart,
  Whilst thou sat on the judgment-seat ?
Who watered thy roses and trained thy vines,
  And kept them from careless feet ?

SECOND.

Nay, that is saddest of all to me,
  That is the saddest of all.
My vines are trailing, my roses are parched.
  My lilies droop and fall.

FIRST.

Go back to thy garden-plot, sweetheart,
  Go back till the evening falls,
And bind thy lilies and train thy vines
  Till for thee the Master calls.
Go make thy garden fair as thou canst,
  Thou workest never alone;
Perchance he whose plot is next to thine
  Will see it and mend his own.
And the next shall copy his, sweetheart,
  Till all grows fair and sweet;
And when the Master comes at eve
  Happy faces His coming shall greet.
Then shall thy joy be full, sweetheart,
  In thy garden so fair to see,
In the Master's voice of praise for all,
  In a look of His own for thee.

THE TWO GLASSES.

C. B. A.

[Recitation for Two Students.]

FIRST.

THERE sat two glasses filled to the brim
On a rich man's table, rim to rim;
One was ruddy and red as blood,
And one was as clear as the crystal flood.
Said the glass of wine to the paler brother:

SECOND.

" Let us tell the tales of the past to each other;
I can tell of a banquet and revel and mirth,
Where the proudest and grandest souls on earth
Fell under my touch as though struck by blight;
For I was a king, and I ruled in might;
From the heads of kings I have torn the crown,
From the height of fame I have hurled men down,
I have blasted many an honored name;
I have taken virtue and given shame;
I have made the arm of the driver fail,
And sent the train from the iron rail;
I have made good ships go down at sea,
And the shrieks of the lost were sweet to me;
For they said, 'Behold, how great you be!
Fame, strength, wealth, genius before you fall,
And your might and power are over all.'
Ho! ho! pale brother," laughed the wine,
" Can you boast of deeds as great as mine?"

FIRST.

Said the water-glass: " I cannot boast
Of a king dethroned, or a murdered host;
But I can tell of a heart once sad,
By my crystal drops made light and glad;

7

Of thirsts I've quenched, and brows I've laved;
Of hands I have cooled, and souls I have saved;
I have slept in the sunshine and dropped from the sky,
And everywhere gladdened the landscape and eye;
I have eased the hot forehead of fever and pain,
I have made the parched meadows grow fertile with grain;
I can tell of the powerful wheel of the mill,
That ground out the flour and turned at my will;
I can tell of manhood debased by you,
That I have lifted and crowned anew.
I cheer, I help, I strengthen and aid;
I gladden the heart of man and maid;
I set the chained wine-captive free,
And all are better for knowing me."

SECOND.

These are the tales they told each other,
The glass of wine and its paler brother,
As they sat together, filled to the brim,
On the rich man's table, rim to rim.

THE SORROW OF THE SEA.

Concert.   I STOOD on the shore of the beautiful sea,
            And the billows were rolling wild and free;
            Onward they came with unfailing force,
            Then backward turned in their restless course.
            Ever and ever they rose and fell,
            With heaving and surging and mighty swell:
            Ever and ever sounded their roar,
            Foaming and dashing against the shore.

Solo.   Oh, when shall the ocean's troubled breast
            Calmly and quietly sink to rest ?
            When shall the waves' wild murmurs cease
            And the mighty waters be hushed in peace ?

Concert. It cannot be quiet; it cannot rest.
There must be heaving on ocean's breast,
The tide must ebb and the tide must flow
While the changing seasons come and go.
Oh, strangely glorious, beautiful sea,
Sounding forever mysteriously,
Why are thy billows still rolling on
With that wild and sad and musical tone?
Why is there never repose for thee
O mighty, murmuring, sounding sea?

Solo. Then the ocean's voice I seemed to hear,
Mournfully, solemnly sounding near,
Telling of loved ones buried there,
Of the dying shriek and the dying prayer;
Telling of hearts still watching in vain
For those who shall never come back again;
Oh, no! the ocean can never rest
With such secrets hidden within its breast.
But a day shall come, a blessed day,
When earthly sorrow shall pass away,
When the hour of anguish shall turn to peace,
And even the roar of the waves shall cease.

Concert. But, oh! thou glorious, beautiful sea,
There is health, and joy, and delight in thee.
Solemnly, sweetly, I hear thy voice
Bidding me weep and yet rejoice:
Weep for the loved ones buried beneath,
Rejoice in Him who has conquered death;
Weep for the sorrowing, tempest-tossed,
Rejoice in Him who has saved the lost;
Weep for the sin and sorrow of strife,
Rejoice in the hope of eternal life!

THE DEATH OF OUR ALMANAC.

REV. HENRY WARD BEECHER.

[Selection for Twelve Students.]

January. Darkness and light reign alike. Snow is on the ground, cold is in the air. The winter is blossoming in frost-flowers. Old sounds are silent in the forest and in the air. Insects are dead, birds are gone, leaves have perished. So hath God wiped out the past; so hath he spread the earth, like an unwritten page, for a new year.

February. As the month wears on its silent work begins, though storms rage. The earth is hidden yet, but not dead. The sun is drawing near. He whispers words of deliverance into the ears of every sleeping seed and root that lies beneath the snow. The day opens, but the night shuts the earth with its frost-lock; but day steadily gains upon the night.

March. The conflict is more turbulent, but the victory is gained. The world awakes. There come voices from long-hidden birds. The smell of the soil is in the air. The sullen ice, retreating from open field and all sunny places, has slunk to the north of every fence and rock. The knolls and banks that face the east or south sigh for release, and begin to lift up a thousand tiny palms.

April. The singing month. Many voices of many birds call for resurrection over the graves of flowers, and they come forth. Go, see what they have lost. What have ice, and snow, and storm done unto them? How did they fall into the earth, stripped and bare? How did they come forth, opening and glorified? Is it, then, so fearful a thing to lie in the grave? In its wild career, shaking and scourged of storms through its orbit, the earth has scattered away no treasures. The Hand that governs in April governed in January. You have not lost what God has only hidden. You lose nothing in struggle, in trial, in bitter distress.

May. O Flower-month! perfect the harvests of flowers. Be not niggardly. Search out the cold and resentful nooks that refused the sun, casting back its rays from disdainful ice, and plant flowers even there. There is goodness in the worst. There is warmth in the coldest. The silent, hopeful, unbreathing sun, that will not fret or despond, but carries a placid brow through the unwrinkled heavens, at length conquers the very rocks, and lichens grow and inconspicuously blossom. What shall not Time do, that carries in its bosom Love?

June. Rest! This is the year's bower. Sit down within it. The winds bring perfume, the forests sing to thee, the earth shows thee all her treasures. The air is all sweetness. The storms are but as flocks of mighty birds that spread their wings and sing in the high heaven. The earth cries to the heavens, "God is here!" The heavens cry to the earth, "God is here!" The land claims him, and his footsteps are upon the sea. O sunny joys of sunny June, how soon will you be scorched by the eager months coming burning from the equator!

July. Rouse up! The temperate heats that filled the air are raging forward to glow and overfill the earth. There are deep and unreached places for whose sake the probing sun pierces down its glowing hands. The earth shall drink of the heat before she knows her nature or

her strength. Then shall she bring forth to the uttermost the treasures of her bosom. For there are things
hidden far down, and the deep things of life are not
known till the fire reveals them.

August. Reign, thou Fire-month! Neither shalt
thou destroy the earth which frosts and ice could not
destroy. The vines droop, the trees stagger, but every
night the dew pities them. This is the rejoicing month
for joyful insects, the most populous and the happiest
month. The air is resonant of insect orchestras, each
one carrying his part in nature's grand harmony. August, thou art the ripeness of the year, the glowing center of the great circle.

September. There are thoughts in thy heart of death.
Thou art doing a secret work, and heaping up treasures
for another year. The unborn infant-buds which thou
art tending are more than all the living leaves. Thy
robes are luxuriant, but worn with softened pride. More
dear, less beautiful than June, thou art the heart's
month. Not till the heats of summer are gone, while
all its growths remain, do we know the fullness of life.
Thy hands are stretched out, and clasp the glowing palm
of August, and the fruit-smelling hand of October.
Thou dividest them asunder, and art thyself molded of
them both.

October. Orchard of the year! Bend thy boughs to
the earth, redolent of glowing fruit! Ripened seeds
shake in their pods. Apples drop in the stillest hours.
Leaves begin to let go when no wind is out, and swing
in long waverings to the earth, which they touch without sound, and lie looking up, till winds rake them and
heap them in fence-corners. When the gales come
through the trees, the yellow leaves trail, like sparks at

night behind the flying engine. The woods are thinner, so that we can see the heavens plainer, as we lie dreaming on the yet warm moss by the singing spring. The days are calm. The nights are tranquil. The year's work is done. She walks in gorgeous apparel, looking upon her long labor, and her serene eye saith, "It is good."

November. Patient watcher, thou art asking to lay down thy tasks. Life to thee, now, is only a task accomplished. In the night-time thou liest down, and the messengers of winter deck thee with hoar-frosts for thy burial. The morning looks upon thy jewels, and they perish while it gazes. Wilt thou not come, O December?

December. Silently the month advances. There is nothing to destroy, but much to bury. Bury, then, thou snow, that slumberously fallest through the still air, the hedgerows of leaves! Muffle thy cold wool about the feet of shivering trees! Bury all that the year hath known, and let thy brilliant stars, that never shine as they do in thy frostiest nights, behold the work! But know, O month of destruction, that in thy constellation is set that Star whose rising is the sign, for evermore, that there is life in death! Thou art the month of resurrection. In thee the Christ came. Every star that looks down upon thy labor and toil of burial knows that all things shall come forth again. Storms shall sob themselves to sleep. Silence shall find a voice. Death shall live, Life shall rejoice, Winter shall break forth and blossom into Spring, Spring shall put on her glorious apparel and be called Summer. It is life! it is life! through the whole year!

Two Epitaphs.

[The following can be read by a class in concert, or by two sections of a class. It is a fine exercise in transition from soft to loud Force, slow to quick Time, low to high Pitch, minor to major Inflection.]

I.
" Think of Death !" the grave-stones say,—
" Peace to Life's mad striving !"

II.
But the church-yard daisies,—" Nay,
Think of Living !"

"Think of Life !" the sunbeams say,
O'er the dial flying;

I.
But the slanting shadows,—" Nay,
Think of Dying !"

" Think of Death !" the night birds say,
On the storm-blast driving;

II.
But the building swallows,—" Nay,
Think of Living !"

" Think of Life !" the broad winds say,
Through the old trees sighing;

I.
But the whirling leaf-dance,—"Nay,
Think of Dying !"

" Think of Death !" the sad bells say,
Fateful record giving;

II.
Clash the merry Yule-peal,—" Nay,
Think of Living !"

Concert.   Dying, Living, glad or loath,
On God's Rood relying;
Pray He fit us all for both—
Living, Dying !   *From the German.*

THE CATARACT OF LODORE.

ROBERT SOUTHEY.

[For Solo and Concert Recitation.]

[Variations in Force, Time, Pitch, Quality, Staccato and Legato effect, to be made according to the idea expressed by the different words.]

Solo.

" How does the water come down at Lodore ?"
My little boy asked me
Thus, once on a time,
And moreover he tasked me
To tell him in rhyme.
Anon at the word
There first came one daughter,
And then came another
To second and third
The request of their brother,
And to hear how the water came down at Lodore,
So I told them in rhyme, for of rhymes I had store,
And 'twas in my vocation
For their recreation,
That so I should sing;
Because I was Laureate to them and the King.

Solo.

From its sources which well
In the tarn on the fell;
Through moss and through brake
It runs and it creeps
For a while till it sleeps
In its own little lake;
It runs through the reeds and away it proceeds
Through meadow and glade, in sun and in shade,
And through the wood-shelter, among crags in its flurry
Helter-skelter, hurry-skurry !
The cataract strong then plunges along,
Striking and raging as if a war waging
Its caverns and rocks among.

Concert.

Rising and leaping,
Sinking and creeping,
Flying and flinging,
Writhing and ringing,
Spouting and frisking,
Turning and twisting,—

Solo.

Dizzying and deafening the ear with its sound.

Concert.

And shocking and rocking,
And darting and parting,
And rattling and battling,
And shaking and quaking,
And pouring and roaring,
And waving and raving,
And dropping and hopping,
And working and jerking,
And moaning and groaning.
And falling and brawling and sprawling,
And sprinkling and twinkling and wrinkling,
And sounding and bounding and rounding,
And bubbling and rumbling and tumbling,
And clattering and battering and shattering.
And rushing and flushing and brushing and gushing,
And flapping and rapping and clapping and slapping,
And curling and whirling and furling and twirling,
And thumping and plumping and bumping and jumping,
And dashing and flashing and splashing and crashing—

Solo.

And so never ending, but always descending,
Sounds and motions for ever and ever are blending
All at once, and all o'er, with a mighty uproar,
And this way the water comes down at Lodore.

CAVALRY SONG.

EDMUND C. STEDMAN.

[For Boys' Recitation.]

I.

OUR good steeds snuff the winter air,
Our pulses with their purpose tingle;
The foeman's fires are twinkling there;
He leaps to hear our sabers jingle.

· HALT !

Each carbine send its whizzing ball;
Now cling ! clang ! forward, all,
Into the fight !

II.

Dash on beneath the smoking dome;
Through level lightnings gallop nearer !
One look to Heaven. No thoughts of home;
The guidons that we bear are dearer.

CHARGE !

Cling ! clang ! forward, all !
Heaven help those whose horses fall !
Cut left and right !

III.

They flee before our fierce attack !
They fall ! they spread in broken surges.
Now, comrades, bear our wounded back,
And leave the foeman to his dirges.

WHEEL !

The bugles sound the swift recall;
Cling ! clang ! backward, all!
Home, and good-night !

RECITATIONS FOR MUSIC.

THE ANGELUS.

FRANCES L. MACE.

[For pianissimo musical accompaniment.]

RING soft across the dying day,
  Angelus !
Across the amber-tinted bay,
The meadow flushed with sunset ray,—
Ring out, and float, and melt away,
  Angelus.

The day of toil seems long ago,
  Angelus;
While through the deepening vesper glow,
Far up where holy lilies blow,
Thy beckoning bell-notes rise and flow,
  Angelus.

Through dazzling curtains of the west,
  Angelus !
We see a shrine in roses dressed,
And lifted high in vision blest,
Our very heart-throb is confessed,
  Angelus.

Oh, has an angel touched the bell,
  Angelus ?
For now upon its parting swell
All sorrow seems to sing farewell,
There falls a peace no words can tell,
  Angelus !

HOPE'S SONG.

HELEN M. WINSLOW.

THE golden dreams of youth
Assume a guise of truth
   Which age keeps never,
  For Hope's voice singeth ever,
" Oh, youth and strong endeavor,
  Can win the highest good forever."

Love's subtle intuition
Divines life's glad fruition,
   Distrusting never;
  And sweetly Hope sings ever,
" True love and sweet endeavor
  Shall hold the highest good forever."

Love's sacred tryst is broken,
Heart-breaking words are spoken
   Her bonds to sever;
  But still Hope singeth ever,
" Brave heart and strong endeavor
  Must find the highest good forever."

Pale hands are crossed in death;
Gone is the quivering breath;
   And still a low voice never
  Stops echoing, echoing ever,
" Brave heart and strong endeavor
  Have won the highest good forever."

THE SUNRISE NEVER FAILED US YET.

MRS. CELIA THAXTER.

UPON the sadness of the sea
The sunset broods regretfully;
From the far, lonely spaces, slow
Withdraws the wistful after-glow.

So out of life the splendor dies;
So darken all the happy skies;
So gathers twilight, cold and stern—
But overhead the planets burn.

And up the east another day
Shall chase the bitter dark away;
What though our eyes with tears be wet?
The sunrise never failed us yet!

The blush of dawn may yet restore
Our light, and hope, and joy, once more.
Sad soul, take comfort, nor forget
That sunrise never failed us yet!

————◆————

A WINTER SONG.

[With light, running *staccato* and *legato* accompaniments.]

OH, summer has the roses
    And the laughing, light south wind,
    And the merry meadows lined
With dewy, dancing posies;
    But winter has the sprites
    And the witching frosty nights.

Oh, summer has the splendor
    Of the corn-fields wide and deep,
    Where the scarlet poppies sleep
And wary shadows wander;
    But winter fields are rare
    With diamonds everywhere.

Oh, summer has the wild bees,
    And the ringing, singing note
    In the robin's tuneful throat,
And the leaf-talk in the trees;
    But winter has the chime
    Of the merry Christmas time.

Oh, summer has the luster
    Of the sunbeams warm and bright,
    And rains that fall at night
Where reeds and lilies cluster;
    But deep in winter's snow
    The fires of Christmas glow.

                        St. Nicholas.

—◆—

THE CONCERT REHEARSAL.

WOLSTAN DIXEY.

OH, it was a musical old Beetle !
    And oh, it was a honey-throated Bee !
But the dandified young Hopper,
He couldn't sing it proper.
    And the Cricket—out of tune was he.

They sung and they sung,
And the harebells swung
    A tinkling *obligato* in the breeze;
While the Beetle, singing-master,
Tried to make them sing it faster,
    By patting off the *tempo* on his knees.

And oh ! it was a Robin overheard them,
    Who happened out a-walking in the glade,
And he laughed in every feather
When they tried to sing together
    At the funny little noises that they made.

He listened and he listened,
And his eyes they fairly glistened
   As the Bee so sweetly bumbled out the air;
But the Cricket struck another,
And the Robin thought he'd smother
   Trying not to let them know that he was there.

Then oh, the Bee declared that " It was shameful !"
   And angrily sipped honey from a comb;
" She was ruining her throat
And wouldn't sing another note
   Until the others studied it at home !"

The Cricket said that he
Never *could* keep in the key
   When the wind was blowing that way from the south,
And young Hopper made excuses
In reply to these abuses,
   That he had too much molasses in his mouth.

Then oh ! the beetle-headed old conductor
   Arose and made a few remarks in turn;
" The soprano is so vicious
And affairs so unpropitious,
   The best thing we can do is to adjourn.

" Taking everything together,
   The molasses and the weather,
     And the fact that we can't any of us sing,
There is quite sufficient reason
That we wait another season
   And postpone our little concert till the spring !"

ROCK OF AGES.

[The quoted words can be either sung or recited. The melody should be played through once before the beginning of the recitation. The accompaniment, *pianissimo*, should run through the entire poem, being definite, and *piano* only on the quoted lines.]

" ROCK of ages, cleft for me,"
    Thoughtlessly the maiden sung,
Fell the words unconsciously
    From her girlish, gleeful tongue ;
Sang as little children sing ;
    Sang as sing the birds in June ;
Fell the words like light leaves down
    On the current of the tune—
" Rock of ages, cleft for me,
    Let me hide myself in Thee."

" Let me hide myself in Thee,"—
    Felt her soul no need to hide ;
Sweet the song as song could be,
    And she had no thought beside.
All the words unheedingly
    Fell from lips untouched by care,
Dreaming not that they might be
    On some other lips a prayer—
" Rock of ages, cleft for me,
    Let me hide myself in Thee."

" Rock of ages, cleft for me,"
    'Twas a woman sung them now,
Pleadingly and prayerfully ;
    Every word her heart did know.
Rose the song, as a storm-tossed bird
    Beats with weary wings the air ;
Every note with sorrow stirred—
    Every syllable a prayer—
" Rock of ages, cleft for me,
    Let me hide myself in Thee."

8

" Rock of ages, cleft for me,"
   Lips grown aged sung the hymn
Trustingly and tenderly—
   Voice grown weak and eyes grown dim.
" Let me hide myself in Thee,"
   Trembling though the voice and low,
Rose the sweet strain peacefully
   Like a river in its flow.
Sang as only they can sing
   Who life's thorny paths have passed;
Sang as only they can sing
   Who behold the promised rest—
" Rock of ages, cleft for me,
   Let me hide myself in Thee."

" Rock of ages, cleft for me,"
   Sung above a coffin-lid;
Underneath all restfully
   All life's joys and sorrows hid.
Nevermore, O storm-tossed soul,
   Nevermore, from wind or tide,
Nevermore from billows' roll
   Wilt thou need thyself to hide.
Could the sightless, sunken eyes,
   Closed beneath the soft gray hair,
Could the mute and stiffened lips
   Move again in pleading prayer—
Still, aye still, the words would be,
" Let me hide myself in Thee."

POETS' BIRTHDAYS.

THE BLESSING OF THE POETS.—I think it a very great boon which Heaven bestows on any nation when it sends a real poet among the people, like Longfellow or Whittier. I can't understand why we take the gift so coldly. In some of the poems of Whittier you can almost hear the rustling of the leaves of the old family Bible, and in Longfellow's lines you can listen to the rain on your roof, as you heard it while lying in your chamber in your childhood. It really seems to me that the whole poetic atmosphere of our time has been filled with a new fragrance by Whittier and Longfellow. They have taught us to prize afresh the loftiest virtues and the lowliest charities. Well may they indeed be called "Our Poets of the Household." You may call them primary or secondary, if you choose; but their motive-power remains unquenchable and unchallengeable, and their words are graven in the hearts all over the human world.—JAMES T. FIELDS.

WILLIAM CULLEN BRYANT.
Born Nov. 3, 1794. Died June 12, 1878.

WILLIAM CULLEN BRYANT.

FITZ-GREENE HALLECK.

BRYANT, whose songs are thoughts that bless
  The heart,—its teachers and its joy,—
As mothers blend with their caress
Lessons of truth and gentleness
  And virtue for the listening boy.
Spring's lovelier flowers for many a day
Have blossomed on his wandering way;
Beings of beauty and decay,
  They slumber in their autumn tomb;
But those that graced his own Green River
  And wreathed the lattice of his home,
  Charmed by his song from mortal doom,
Bloom on, and will bloom on forever.

BRYANT had a wonderful memory. His familiarity with the English poets was such that when at sea, where he was always too ill to read much, he would beguile the time by recit ng page after page from favorite poems. He assured me that however long the voyage, he had never exhausted his resources. He was scarcely less familiar with the languages and literatures of Germany, France and Spain, Greece and Rome. He spoke all living languages except the Greek with facility and correctness.—JOHN BIGELOW.

THE name of Bryant cannot be mentioned by any friend to American letters without respect as well as admiration. The hold that he has on the profoundest feelings of his countrymen is to be referred to the genuineness, delicacy, depth, and purity of his sentiment. He is so genuine that he testifies to nothing in scenery or human life of which he has not had a direct personal consciousness. He follows the primitive bias of his nature rather than the caprices of fancy. His compositions always leave the impression of having been born, not manufactured or made.—EDWIN P. WHIPPLE.

IT IS the glory of this man that his character outshone even his great talent and his large fame. Distinguished equally for his native gifts and his consummate culture, his poetic inspiration and his exquisite art, he is honored and loved to-day even more for his stainless purity of life, his unswerving rectitude of will, his devotion to the higher interests of his race, his unfeigned patriotism, and his broad humanity.—REV. HENRY W. BELLOWS.

WHEN Cooper died, the restless city paused to hear Bryant's words of praise and friendship. When Irving followed Cooper, all hearts turned to Bryant. Now Bryant has followed Cooper and Irving, the last of that early triumvirate of American literature. The broad and simple outline of his character and career had become universally familiar like a mountain or the sea. A patriarch of our literature, the oldest of our poets, he felt the magic of human sympathy, the impulse of his country, the political genius of his race, and was a public political leader.—GEORGE WILLIAM CURTIS.

A BRYANT ALPHABET.

ALIKE, beneath thine eye,
The deeds of darkness and of light are done;
  High towards the star-lit sky
Towns blaze, the smoke of battle blots the sun.
Hymn to the North Star.

Beneath the forest's skirt I rest,
  Whose branching pines rise dark and high,
And hear the breezes of the West
  Among the thread-like foliage sigh.
The West Wind.

Calm rose afar the city spires, and thence
  Came the deep murmur of its throng of men;
And as its grateful odors met thy sense,
  They seemed the perfumes of thy native fen.
To a Mosquito.

Darker—still darker ! the whirlwinds bear
The dust of the plains to the middle air;
And hark to the crashing, long and loud,
Of the chariot of God, in the thunder-cloud !
The Hurricane.

Enough of drought has parched the year, and scared
The land with dread of famine.   Autumn, yet,
Shall make men glad with unexpected fruits.
> *The Conjunction of Jupiter and Venus.*

Far back in the ages,
The plow with wreaths was crowned;
The hands of kings and sages
Entwined the chaplet round.
> *Ode for an Agricultural Celebration.*

Glide on in your beauty, ye youthful spheres,
To weave the dance that measures the years;
Glide on, in the glory and gladness sent
To the furthest wall of the firmament.
> *Song of the Stars.*

Hear, Father, hear thy faint afflicted flock
Cry to thee, from the desert and the rock;
While those who seek to slay thy children, hold
Blasphemous worship under roofs of gold.
> *Hymn of the Waldenses.*

I know where the timid fawn abides
In the depths of the shaded dell,
Where the leaves are broad, and the thicket hides
From the eye of the hunter well.
> *An Indian Story.*

Journeying, in long serenity, away
In such a bright, late quiet, would that I
Might wear out life like thee !
> *October.*

Knit they the gentle ties which long
These Sister States were proud to wear,
And forged the kindly links so strong
For idle hands in sport to tear ?
> *Not Yet.*

Lament who will, in fruitless tears,
  The speed with which our moments fly;
I sigh not over vanished years,
  But watch the years that hasten by.
                              The Lapse of Time.

    Might but a little part,
A wandering breath, of that high melody
    Descend into my heart,
    And change it till it be
Transformed and swallowed up, O love, in thee !
                              The Life of the Blessed.

  Not from the sands or cloven rocks,
    Thou rapid Arve ! thy waters flow;
  Nor earth, within her bosom, locks
    Thy dark unfathomed wells below.
                              To the River Arve.

  Oh, deem not they are blest alone
    Whose lives a peaceful tenor keep;
  The Power who pities man has shown
    A blessing for the eyes that weep.
                    " Blessed are they that Mourn."

Peace to the just man's memory; let it grow
Greener with years, and blossom through the flight
Of ages.   *The Ages.*

          ————the great deep
Quivered and shook, as shakes the glimmering air
Above a furnace.   *Sella.*

  Raise, then, the hymn to Death.   Deliverer !
  God hath anointed thee to free the oppressed
  And crush the oppressor.   *Hymn to Death.*

    Seek'st thou the plashy brink
Of weedy lake, or marge of river wide,
Or where the the rocking billows rise and sink
    On the chafed ocean side ?
                              To a Waterfall.

Thou unrelenting Past!
Strong are the barriers round thy dark domain
    And fetters, sure and fast,
Hold all that enter thy unbreathing reign.

The Past.

Upon the mountain's distant head
    With trackless snows forever white,
Where all is still, and cold, and dead,
    Late shines the day's departing light.

" *Upon the Mountain's Distant Head.*"

Violets spring in the soft May shower;
There, in the summer breezes, wave
Crimson phlox and moccasin flower.

The Maiden's Sorrow.

Welcome to grasp of friendly hands; to prayers
Offered where crowds in reverent worship come
Or softly breathed amid the tender cares
And loving inmates of thy quiet home.

The Life that Is.

Alexis calls me cruel;
    The rifted crags that hold
The gathered ice of winter,
    He says, are not more cold.

Song from the Spanish.

Yet these sweet sounds of the early season
    And these fair sights of its sunny days,
Are only sweet when we fondly listen,
    And only fair when we fondly gaze.

An Invitation to the Country.

Leave Zelinda altogether,
    Whom thou leavest oft and long,
And in the life thou lovest
    Forget whom thou dost wrong.

The Alcayde of Molina.

THE THIRD OF NOVEMBER.

ON my cornice linger the ripe, black grapes ungathered;
  Children fill the groves with the echoes of their glee,
Gathering tawny chestnuts, and shouting when beside them
  Drop the heavy fruit of the tall black walnut tree.

Glorious are the woods in their latest gold and crimson,
  Yet our full-leaved willows are in their freshest green,
Such a kindly autumn, so mercifully dealing
  With the growths of summer, I never yet have seen.

Like this kindly season may life's decline come o'er me;
  Past is manhood's summer, the frosty months are here;
Yet be genial airs, and a pleasant sunshine left me,
  Leaf, and fruit, and blossom, to mark the closing year.

THE NIGHT JOURNEY OF A RIVER.

O darkling River ! Through the night I hear
Thy wavelets rippling on the pebbly beach;
I hear thy current stir the rustling sedge
That skirts thy bed; thou intermittest not
Thine everlasting journey, drawing on
A silvery train from many a woodland spring
And mountain brook. The dweller by thy side,
Who moored his little boat upon thy beach,
Though all the waters that upbore it then
Have slid away o'er night, shall find, at noon
Thy channels filled with waters freshly drawn
From distant cliffs and hollows, where the rill
Comes up amid the water-flags. All night
Thou givest moisture to the thirsty roots
Of the lithe willow and overhanging plane,
And cherishest the herbage of thy bank,
Spotted with little flowers, and sendeth up
Perpetually the vapors from thy face,
To steep the hills with dew, or darken heaven
With drifting clouds, that trail the shadowy shower.

THE HURRICANE.

LORD of the winds ! I feel thee nigh,
I know thy breath in the burning sky !
And I wait, with a thrill in every vein,
For the coming of the hurricane !
And lo ! on the wing of the heavy gales,
Through the boundless arch of heaven he sails.
Silent and slow, and terribly strong,
The mighty shadow is borne along,
Like the dark eternity to come;
While the world below, dismayed and dumb,
Through the calm of the thick, hot atmosphere
Looks up at its gloomy folds with fear.

*   *   *   *

He is come ! he is come !   Do ye not behold
His ample robes on the wind unrolled ?
Giant of air ! we bid thee hail !—
How his gray skirts toss in the whirling gale !
How his huge and writhing arms are bent
To clasp the zone of the firmament,
And fold, at length, in their dark embrace,
From mountain to mountain the visible space !

Darker—still darker ! the whirlwinds bear
The dust of the plains to the middle air;
And hark to the crashing, long and loud,
Of the chariot of God in the thunder-cloud !
You may trace its path by the flashes that start
From the rapid wheels where'er they dart,
As the fire-bolts leap to the world below,
And flood the skies with a lurid glow.

GREEN RIVER.

YET pure its waters—its shallows are bright
With colored pebbles and sparkles of light,
And clear the depth where its eddies play,
And dimples deepen and whirl away,
·And the plane-tree's speckled arms o'ershoot
The swifter current that mines its root,
Through whose shifting waves as you walk the hill,
The quivering glimmer of sun and rill
With a sudden flash on the eye is thrown,
Like the ray that streams from the diamond stone !
Oh, loveliest there the spring days come,
With blossoms, and birds, and wild bees' hum;
The flowers of summer are fairest there,
And freshest the breath of the summer air;
And sweetest the golden autumn day
In silence and sunshine glides away.

THE VIOLET.

WHEN birchen buds begin to swell,
   And woods the bluebirds' warble know,
The little violet's modest bell
   Peeps from the last year's leaves below.

Oft in the sunless April day
   Thy early smile has stayed my walk;
But midst the gorgeous blooms of May
   I passed thee on thy humble stalk.

So they who climb to wealth forget
   The friends in darker fortunes tried;
I copied them, but I regret
   That I should ape the ways of pride.

RALPH WALDO EMERSON.

Born May 25, 1803.   Died April 27, 1882.

EMERSON.

MRS. E. C. KINNEY.

DEAR Nature's child, he nestled close to her !
  She to his heart had whispered deeper things
  Than science from the wells of learning brings.
His still small voice the human soul could stir,
  For Nature made him her interpreter.
  And gave her favorite son far-reaching wings;
  He soared and sang as Heaven's lark only sings,
Devout in praise, Truth's truest worshiper.
  With eyes anointed, in his upward flight
  He quick discerned what was divine in men,
  Reading the humblest spirit's tongue aright.
O Prophet, Poet, Leader ! in thy light
  How many saw beyond their natural ken,
  Who follow now the star that led thee then !

EMERSON'S writings call for thought in the reader. They demand that one should stop and ask questions, should translate what one has read into one's own ordinary speech, and inquire again if it is true. No one should read Emerson who is not willing to have his own weakness disclosed to him, and who is not prepared also to test what he finds by a standard which is above both writer and reader.—HORACE E. SCUDDER.

THERE are living organisms so transparent that we can see their hearts beating and their blood flowing through their glassy tissues. So transparent was the life of Emerson; so clearly did the true nature of the man show through it. What he taught others to be he was himself. His deep and sweet humanity won him love and reverence everywhere among those whose natures were capable of responding to the highest manifestations of character.—OLIVER WENDELL HOLMES.

THOUGH Emerson had reached a great age, we were not ready to part with him. He was an important friend, companion, kinsman, fellow-citizen, to the last; a wayfarer everybody was glad to meet; one whose enemy none could continue to be; a charmer whose spell was not to be escaped. With his imagination for an eye, Emerson was a perceiver, and he respected perception in himself and others, being as quick and glad to quote their perceptions as to announce his own. He notes, cites, and lauds every scrap of insight, or ripple of tidings over the ocean that heaves from the unknown shore towards which he sails.—REV. C. A. BARTOL.

EMERSON'S faith in America is justified whether we trust in the capacities of the individual soul, or whether our expectation grows from the promises of a new civilization. America brings together the races of the world as no nation or time ever did before, and Emerson's hope for America may yet be justified by a literature in harmony with the new time.—GEORGE WILLIS COOKE.

LONG, long had we heard in India of his name and reputation. We wondered what manner of man he was. When at last I landed on your continent, how glad I should have been to sit at his feet and unfold before him the tale of our woe and degradation! But he had gone to his rest, and instead of touching his warm hand which had blessed so many pilgrims, I could but kiss the cold dust of his nameless grave at the Concord cemetery.—PROTAP CHUNDER MOZOOMDAR.

AN EMERSON ALPHABET.

ALL right activity is amiable. I never feel that any man occupies my place, but that the reason why I do not have what I wish is, that I want the faculty which entitles. All spiritual or real power makes its own place.

Aristocracy.

By right or wrong,
Lands and goods go to the strong,
Property will brutely draw
Still to the proprietor;
Silver to silver creep and wind,
And kind to kind.

The Celestial Love.

Come see the northwind's masonry:
Out of an unseen quarry evermore
Furnished with tile, the fierce artificer
Curves his white bastions with projected roof.

The Snow-storm.

Do not spare to put novels into the hands of young people as an occasional holiday and experiment; but, above all, good poetry in all kinds, epic, tragedy, lyric.

Education.

Europe has always owed to Oriental genius its divine impulses. What those holy bards said, all sane men found agreeable and true.—*Address to Divinity Students.*

> For Nature ever faithful is
> To such as trust her faithfulness.
>
> *Woodnotes.*

> Gentle pilgrim, if thou know
> The gamut old of Pan,
> And how the hills began,
> The frank blessings of the hill
> Fall on thee, as fall they will.
>
> *Monadnoc.*

He is great who confers the most benefits. He is base—and that is the one base thing in the universe—to receive favors and render none.—*Compensation.*

> Insect lover of the sun,
> Joy of thy dominion;
> Sailor of the atmosphere,
> Swimmer through the waves of air.
>
> *The Humble-bee.*

Jesus astonishes and overpowers sensual people. They cannot unite Him to history, or reconcile Him with themselves.—*History.*

> Knowest thou that wove yon wood-bird's nest
> Of leaves, and feathers from her breast?
> Or how the fish outbuilt her shell,
> Painting with morn each annual shell?
>
> *The Problem.*

Let a man control the habit of expense.   Let him see
that as much wisdom may be expended on a private
economy as on an empire, and as much wisdom be drawn
from it.—*Prudence.*

> Man was made of solid earth,
> Child and brother from his birth;
> Tethered by a liquid cord
> Of blood through veins of kindred poured.
> > *The Celestial Love.*

No man can learn what he has not preparation for
learning, however near to his eyes is the object.   A
chemist may tell his most precious secrets to a carpenter,
and he shall never be the wiser.—*Spiritual Laws.*

> One harvest from thy field
> Homeward brought the oxen strong;
> A second crop thine acres yield
> Which I gather in a song.   *The Apology.*

People say sometimes, "See what I have overcome ;
see how cheerful I am ; see how completely I have triumphed over these black events."   Not if they still remind me of the black event.—*Circles.*

> Queen of things ! I dare not die
> In Being's deeps past ear and eye;
> Lest there I find the same deceiver
> And be the sport of Fate forever.
> > *Ode to Beauty.*

> River and rose and crag and bird,
> Frost and sun and eldest night,
> To me their aid preferred,
> To me their comfort plight.   *Hermione.*

Spartans, stoics, heroes, saints, and gods use a short and positive speech. They are never off their centers. As soon as they swell and paint and find truth not enough for them, softening of the brain has already begun.—*The Superlative.*

> Teach me your mood, O patient stars !
> Who climb each night the ancient sky,
> Leaving on space no shade, no scars,
> No trace of age, no fear to die. *The Poet.*

Upborne and surrounded as we are by this all-creating nature, soft and fluid as a cloud or the air, why should we be such hard pedants and magnify a few forms ?
History.

> Virtue runs before the Muse,
> And defies her skill;
> She is rapt, and doth refuse
> To wait a painter's will. *Loss and Gain.*

Wise, cultivated, genial conversation is the last flower of civilization, and the best result which life has to offer us,—a cup for gods, which has no repentance. Conversation is our account of ourselves.—*Woman.*

EXTRACT FROM " COMPENSATION.

THE history of persecution is a history of endeavors to cheat nature, to make water run up-hill, to twist a rope of sand. It makes no difference whether the actors be many or one, a tyrant or a mob. The martyr cannot be dishonored. Every lash inflicted is a tongue of flame ; every prison, a more illustrious abode ; every burned

9

book or house enlightens the world ; every suppressed
or expunged word reverberates through the earth from
side to side. Hours of sanity and consideration are always arriving to communities as to individuals, when
the truth is seen, and the martyrs are justified.

THE CONCORD FIGHT.

BY the rude bridge that arched the flood,
　Their flag to April's breeze unfurled.
Here once the embattled farmers stood
　And fired the shot heard round the world.

The foe has long in silence slept:
　Alike the conqueror silent sleeps ; ·
And time the ruined bridge has swept
　Down the dark stream which seaward creeps.

On this green bank, by this soft stream,
　We set to-day a votive stone,
That memory may their deed redeem,
　When like our sires our sons are gone.

EXTRACT FROM "WORKS AND DAYS."

'TIS a fine fable for the advantage of character over
talent, the Greek legend of the strife of Jove and Phœbus. Phœbus challenged the gods and said, "Who will
outshoot the far-darting Apollo?" Zeus said, "I will."
Mars shook the lots in his helmet, and that of Apollo
leaped out first. Apollo stretched his bow and shot his
arrow into the extreme west. Then Zeus arose, and with
one stride cleared the whole distance, and said, "Where
shall I shoot? There is no space left." So the bow-
man's prize was adjudged to him who drew no bow.

ART.

GIVE to barrows, trays, and pans
Grace and glimmer of romance;
Bring the moonlight into noon
Hid in gleaming piles of stone;
On the city's pavèd street
Plant gardens lined with lilac sweet,
Let spouting fountains cool the air,
Singing in the sun-baked square;
Let statue, picture, park, and hall,
Ballad, flag, and festival,
The past restore, the day adorn,
And make each morrow a new morn.
'Tis the privilege of Art
Thus to play its cheerful part.

THE RHODORA.

RHODORA ! if the sages ask thee why
This charm is wasted on the earth and sky,
Tell them, dear, that if eyes were made for seeing
Then beauty is its own excuse for being.

Why thou wert there, O rival of the rose !
I never thought to ask ; I never knew,
But in my simple ignorance suppose
The self-same Power that brought me here, brought you.

OLIVER WENDELL HOLMES.
Born Aug. 29, 1809.

OUR AUTOCRAT.
JOHN G. WHITTIER.

HIS laurels fresh from song and lay,
  Romance and art, so young withal
At heart, we scarcely dare to say
  We keep his seventieth festival.

His still the keen analysis
  Of men and moods, electric wit,
Free play of mirth, and tenderness
  To heal the slightest wound from it.

And his the pathos touching all
  Life's sins and sorrows and regrets,
Its hopes and fears, its final call
  And rest beneath the violets.

His sparkling surface scarce betrays
  The thoughtful tide beneath it rolled,
The wisdom of the latter days
  And tender memories of the old.

Though now unnumbered guests surround
  The table that he rules at will,
Its autocrat, however crowned,
  Is but our friend and comrade still.

Long may he live to sing for us
  The songs that stay the flight of time,
And like his Chambered Nautilus,
  To holier heights of beauty climb.

Dec. 3, 1879.

I THINK that none of us can understand the meaning and scope of Dr. Holmes's writings unless we have observed that the main work of his life has been to study and teach an exact science, the noble science of anatomy. And let us honor him to-day, not forgetting, as they can never be forgotten, his poems, his essays, as a noble representative of the profession of the scientific student and teacher.—CHARLES W. ELIOT.

WHAT one does easily is apt to be his forte, though years may pass before he finds this out. Holmes's early pieces, mostly college-verse, were better of their kind than those of a better kind written in youth by some of his contemporaries. The humbler the type, the sooner the development. The young poet had the aid of a suitable habitat; life at Harvard was the precise thing to bring out his talent. There was nothing of the hermit-thrush in him; his temper was not of the withdrawing and reflective kind, nor moodily introspective,—it throve on fellowship, and he looked to his mates for an audience as readily as they to him for a toast-master.— FRANCES H. UNDERWOOD.

ONE finds nowhere in Holmes's volumes crude and unformed thoughts. He writes as clearly as he thinks. His sentences come from his pen clean-cut. The language of his prose is pure classical English. His style is simple, direct, forcible; affluent, in the sense that it apparently never fails to come spontaneously at need, and in the fittest form; but not exuberant to the obscuring of the thought. Whether he be discussing a medical thesis or reading a lyric to classmates and literary friends at an anniversary dinner, or sketching character in the romance, or playing the autocrat at the breakfast-table, it is sure to be found acting effectively on those who hear or read them.—REV. RAY PALMER.

———◆———

IT is as a writer of humorous poetry that Holmes excels. His non-humorous poems are full of beautiful passages, as we shall see, but they have not the same unique flavor of originality. In one of the great London papers it was editorially stated, not long since, that no contemporary American writer had so amused and instructed the insular mind as Holmes had done. The one most charming feature of his printed and spoken conversation is that he establishes a relation of sympathy between himself and his listeners, by expressing for them those common, every-day thoughts that we all think but rarely say.—WM. SLOANE KENNEDY.

———◆———

THE grace and gayety, the pathos and melody, the wit, the earnestness and shrewd sense of his writings, have given Holmes a place, and a sunny place, in the popular heart. On his happy birthday it was not Boston that sat at table, but the whole country. It was not a town meeting, but a national congress. The Autocrat is not a mayor, but an emperor, and the toast of the day was the toast of appreciative hearts and generous souls far beyond the sound of the Atlantic. "The Autocrat of the Breakfast-table; O king, live forever!" —GEO. WM. CURTIS.

A HOLMES ALPHABET.

ALONG its front no sabers shine,
   No blood-red pennons wave;
Its banner bears the single line,
   "Our duty is to save."   *The Two Armies.*

Bring bellows for the panting winds,
   Hang up a lantern by the moon;
And give the nightingale a fife,
   And lend the eagle a balloon.
              The Meeting of the Dryads.

Child of the plowshare, smile;
   Boy of the counter, grieve not,
Though muses round thy trundle-bed
   Their broidered tissue weave not.
                   The Poet's Lot.

Dear friends, who are listening so sweetly the while
With your lips double-reefed in a snug little smile,
I leave you two fables, both drawn from the deep,—
The shells you can drop, but the pearls you may keep.
                 Verses for After-dinner.

Each moment fainter wave the fields
   And wider rolls the sea;
The mist grows dark,—the sun goes down,—
   Day breaks,—and where are we ?
                   Departed Days.

FLOWERS will bloom over and over again in poems as
in the summer fields, to the end of time, always old
and always new. Why should we be more shy of repeating ourselves than the spring be tired of blossoms
or the night of stars ?—*The Autocrat of the Breakfast-
table.*

God of all nations ! Sovereign Lord !
In Thy dread name we draw the sword,
We lift the starry flag on high
That fills with light our stormy sky.
                              Army Hymn.

How patient Nature smiles at Fame !
    The weeds that strewed the victor's way,
Feed on his dust to shroud his name,
    Green where his proudest towers decay.
                    A Roman Aqueduct.

It is likely that the language will shape itself by larger forces than phonography and dictionary-making. You may spade up the ocean as much as you like, and harrow it afterward if you can, but the moon will still lead the tides, and the winds will form their surface.— *The Professor at the Breakfast-table.*

Joy smiles in the fountain,
    Health flows in the rills,
As their ribbons of silver
    Unwind from the hills.
            Song for a Temperance Dinner.

Know old Cambridge ?   Hope you do.
Born there ?   Don't say so !   I was too.
                    Parson Turrell's Legacy.

Let each unhallowed cause that brings
    The stern destroyer cease,
Thy flaming angel fold his wings
    And seraphs whisper Peace !
                        Parting Hymn.

Many ideas grow better when transplanted into another mind than in the one where they sprang up. That which was a weed in one intelligence becomes a flower in the other. A flower, on the other hand, may dwindle down to a mere weed by the same change.— *The Poet at the Breakfast-table.*

> None wept,—none pitied;—they who knelt
> At morning by the despot's throne
> At evening dashed the laureled bust
> And spurned the wreaths themselves had strewn.
> *The Dying Seneca.*

> Over the hill-sides the wild knell is tolling,
> From their far hamlets the yeomanry come;
> As through the storm-clouds the thunder-burst rolling,
> Circles the beat of the mustering drum.
> *Lexington.*

> Poor conquered monarch ! though that haughty glance
> Still speaks thy courage unsubdued by time,
> And in the grandeur of thy sullen tread
> Lives the proud spirit of thy burning clime.
> *To a Caged Lion.*

> Questioning all things: Why her Lord had sent her ?
> What were these torturing gifts, and wherefore lent her ?
> Scornful as spirit fallen, its own tormentor.
> *Iris, Her Book.*

> Rain me sweet odors on the air
> And wheel me up my Indian chair,
> And spread some book not overwise
> Flat out before my sleepy eyes.
> *Midsummer.*

> Scenes of my youth ! awake, its slumbering fire !
> Ye winds of Memory, sweep the silent lyre !
> Ray of the past, if yet thou canst appear,
> Break through the clouds of Fancy's waning year.
> *A Metrical Essay.*

Trees as we see them, love them, adore them in the fields, where they are alive, holding their green sun-shades over our heads, talking to us with their hundred thousand whispering tongues, looking down on us with that sweet meekness which belongs to huge but limited organisms.—*The Autocrat of the Breakfast-table.*

> Unscathed, she treads the wreck-piled street
>   Whose narrow gaps afford
> A pathway for her bleeding feet,
>   To seek her absent lord.   *Agnes.*

> Virtue—the guide that men and nations own ;
> And Law—the bulwark that protects her throne;
> And Health—to all its happiest charm that lends,—
> These and their servants, man's untiring friends.
>   *A Modest Request.*

> Wan-visaged thing ! thy virgin leaf
>   To me looks more than deadly pale,
> Unknowing what may stain thee yet,—
>   A poem or a tale.
>   *To a Blank Sheet of Paper.*

"It ain't jest the thing to grease your ex with ile o' vitrul," said the Member.—*The Poet at the Breakfast-table.*

> Ye know not,—but the hour is nigh;
>   Ye will not heed the warning breath;
> No vision strikes your clouded eye,
>   To break the sleep that wakes in death.
>   *The Last Prophecy of Cassandra.*

> " By Zhorzhe !" as friend Sales is accustomed to cry,
>   You tell me they're dead, but I know it's a lie;
>   Is Jackson not President ?   What was't you said ?
>   It can't be; you're joking; what,—all of 'em dead ?
>   *Once More.*

UNDER THE WASHINGTON ELM, CAMBRIDGE.

April 27, 1861.

EIGHTY years have passed, and more,
  Since under the brave old tree ˙
Our fathers gathered in arms, and swore
They would follow the sign their banners bore,
  And fight till the land was free.

  Half of their work was done,
    Half is left to do,—
Cambridge, and Concord, and Lexington !
When the battle is fought and won,
    What shall be told of you ?

  Hark !—'tis the south-wind moans,—
    Who are the martyrs down ?
Ah, the marrow was true in your children's bones
That sprinkled with blood the cursèd stones
    Of the murder-haunted town !

  What if the storm-clouds blow ?
    What if the green leaves fall ?
Better the crashing tempest's throe
Than the army of worms that gnawed below;
    Trample them one and all !

  Then, when the battle is won,
    And the land from traitors free,
Our children shall tell of the strife begun
When Liberty's second April sun
    Was bright on our brave old tree !

THE TWO STREAMS.

BEHOLD the rocky wall
 That down its sloping sides
Pours the swift rain-drops, blending, as they fall
 In rushing river-tides !

Yon stream, whose sources run
 Turned by a pebble's edge,
Is Athabasca, rolling toward the sun
 Through the cleft mountain-ledge.

The slender rill had strayed,
 But for the slanting stone,
To evening's ocean, with the tangled braid
 Of foam-flecked Oregon.

So from the heights of Will
 Life's parting stream descends,
And, as a moment turns its slender rill,
 Each widening torrent bends,—

From the same cradle's side,
 From the same mother's knee,—
One to long darkness and the frozen tide,
 One to the Peaceful Sea.

------◆------

INTERNATIONAL ODE.

OUR FATHERS' LAND.*

GOD bless our Fathers' Land !
Keep her in heart and hand
 One with our own !
From all her foes defend,
Be her brave People's Friend,
On all her realms descend,
 Protect her Throne !

* Sung in unison by twelve hundred children of the public schools, at the visit of the Prince of Wales to Boston, October 18, 1860. Air, " God save the Queen."

Father, with loving care
Guard Thou her kingdom's Heir,
 Guide all his ways:
Thine arm his shelter be,
From him by land and sea
Bid storm and danger flee,
 Prolong his days!

Lord, let War's tempest cease,
Fold the whole Earth in peace
 Under thy wings!
Make all Thy nations one,
All hearts beneath the sun,
Till thou shalt reign alone,
 Great King of kings!

JAMES RUSSELL LOWELL'S BIRTHDAY FESTIVAL.

WE will not speak of years to-night,
 For what have years to bring
But larger floods of love and light,
 And sweeter songs to sing.

Enough for him the silent grasp
 That knits us hand in hand,
And he the bracelet's radiant clasp
 That locks our circling band.

Strength to his hours of manly toil,
 Peace to his starlit dreams!
Who loves alike the furrowed soil,
 The music-haunted streams!

Sweet smiles to keep forever bright
 The sunshine on his lips,
And faith that sees the ring of light
 Round nature's last eclipse.

HENRY WADSWORTH LONGFELLOW.

Born Feb. 27, 1807. Died March 24, 1882.

HENRY WADSWORTH LONGFELLOW.

WILLIAM W. STORY.

A PURE sweet spirit, generous and large
   Was thine, dear poet. Calm, unturbulent,
   Its course along Life's varying ways it went,
Like some broad river on whose happy marge
Are noble groves, lawns, towns—which takes the charge
   Of peaceful freights from inward regions sent
   For human use and help and heart's content,
And bears Love's sunlit sails and Beauty's barge.
So brimming, deepening ever to the sea
   Through gloom and sun, reflecting inwardly
   The ever-changing heavens of day and night,
Thy life flowed on, from all low passions free,
   Filled with high thoughts, charmed into Poesy
   To all the world a solace and delight.

YES, we were warm friends. He was a delightful man and a great poet. Hawthorne, Emerson, Longfellow, and myself were always friends. There were no jealousies between us, and each took a pride in the work and successes of the other. We would exchange notes upon our productions, and if one saw a kindly notice of the other it was always cut out and sent him.—JOHN G. WHITTIER.

THE magnetism of Longfellow's touch lies in the broad humanity of his sympathy which commends his poetry to the universal heart. His artistic sense is so exquisite that each of his poems is a valuable literary study. Longfellow's mind takes a simple, childlike hold of life. His delightful familiarity with the pure literature of all languages and times must rank him among the learned poets.—GEORGE WILLIAM CURTIS.

IT is a singular fact that Longfellow is more popular in England than Tennyson, the laureate. Yet perhaps it is not so very singular. He sings like one whose heart has been warmed at the hearth-stone. There is hardly a line of his but would rhyme with the chirp of the cricket; hearts are hearts whatever blood quickens them, and he has touched the heart as no other poet of his day has. Is there any one whose life is likely to remind us more forcibly of the sublimity of patience, truth, purity, and all the virtues than that of Henry Wadsworth Longfellow?— RICHARD HENRY STODDARD.

A POETICAL atmosphere, an aroma, hung about Longfellow as about no other of our poets. He was associated with memories of the early years of the republic; with the picturesque epoch of our national existence; with the dawn of democratic institutions, with the flushing hope which reddened the sky when the young nation committed itself so cordially to faith in man. His name was seldom spoken except in connection with charity and good-will. And when he died, the sorrow of the greatest and of the least was equally sincere.—REV. OCTAVIUS B. FROTHINGHAM.

Can it be that a man like this is dead? I cannot believe it. Like a lark that sings and soars, and still sings fading out of sight in the blue heavens. I cannot believe that he has gone because he has disappeared from our view. A rounded life was his; his work was done. Where has he gone? We may not know as yet. So far as we are concerned, he has gone, to quote his own words, "into the silent land." We will rejoice that he has left behind him words that will sing their song of trust and hope for many a year to come.—Rev. Minot J. Savage.

A Longfellow Alphabet.

Awake! arise! the hour is late!
    Angels are knocking at thy door!
They are in haste and cannot wait,
    And once departed come no more.
                  A Fragment.

Bear a lily in thy hand;
Gates of brass cannot withstand
One touch of that magic wand.
                  Maidenhood.

Closed was the teacher's task, and with heaven in their hearts
    and their faces
Up rose the children all, and each bowed him, weeping full
    sorely,
Downward to kiss that reverend hand.
            Children of the Lord's Supper.

Day after day we think what she is doing
    In those bright realms of air;
Year after year, her tender steps pursuing,
    Behold her grown more fair.   *Resignation.*

Each heart has its haunted chamber,
Where the silent moonlight falls!
On the floor are mysterious footsteps,
There are whispers along the walls !
The Haunted Chamber.

" Farewell !" the portly landlord cried;
" Farewell !" the parting guests replied,
But little thought that never more
Their feet would pass that threshold o'er.
Tales of a Wayside Inn.

Gone are all the barons bold,
Gone are all the knights and squires;
Gone the abbot, stern and cold,
And the brotherhood of friars.
Oliver Basselin.

How many centuries has it been
About those deserts blown !
How many strange vicissitudes has seen,
How many histories known !
Sand of the Desert.

It sees the ocean to its bosom clasp
The rocks and sea-sand with the kiss of peace,
It sees the wild winds lift it in their grasp,
And hold it up and shake it like a fleece.
The Lighthouse.

Just above yon sandy bar,
As the day grows faint and dimmer,
Lonely and lovely. a single star
Lights the air with a dusky glimmer.
Chrysaor.

Knelt the Black Robe chief with his children, a crucifix fast-
ened
High on the trunk of the tree.   This was their rural chapel.
Evangeline.

Left to myself, I wander as I will,
And as my fancy leads me, through this house;
Nor could I ask a dwelling more complete,
Were I indeed the goddess that he deems me.
The Masque of Pandora.

Month after month passed away, and in autumn the ships of
the merchants
Came with kindred and friends, with cattle and corn for the
Pilgrims. *The Courtship of Miles Standish.*

Nine sisters, beautiful in form and face,
Came from their convent on the shining heights
Of Pierus, the mountain of delights,
To dwell among the people at its base.
The Nine Muses.

"O Cæsar, we who are about to die
Salute you!" was the gladiators' cry
In the arena, standing face to face
With death and with the Roman populace.
Morituri Salutamus.

Peradventure of old, some bard in Ionian Islands,
Walking alone by the sea, hearing the wash of the waves,
Learned the secret from them of the beautiful verse elegiac.
Elegiac Verse.

Quiet, close, and warm,
Sheltered from all molestation,
And recalling by their voices
Youth and travel.
To an Old Danish Song-book.

River! that in silence windest
Through the meadows, bright and free,
Till at length thy rest thou findest
In the bosom of the sea!
To the River Charles.

Sudden and swift, a whistling ball
Came out of a wood, and the voice was still;
Something I heard in the darkness fall,
And for a moment my blood grew chill.

Killed at the Ford.

Thou standest, like imperial Charlemagne,
Upon thy bridge of gold; thy royal hand
Outstretched with benedictions o'er the land,
Blessing the farms through all thy vast domains.

Autumn.

Up soared the lark into the air,—
A shaft of song, a winged prayer,
As if a soul, released from pain,
Were flying back to heaven again.

The Sermon of St. Francis.

Visions of the days departed, shadowy phantoms filled my
brain;
They who live in history only seemed to walk the earth again.

The Belfry of Bruges.

Whereunto is money good?
Who has it not wants hardihood;
Who has it has much trouble and care;
Who once has had it has despair.

Poetic Aphorisms.

" Excelsior !"

Excelsior.

Youth is lovely, age is lonely,
Youth is fiery, age is frosty;
You bring back the days departed,
And the beautiful Wenonah.

Hiawatha.

Zeal was stronger than fear or love.

Tales of a Wayside Inn.

MUSINGS.

[An early poem, not usually published.]

I SAT by my window one night,
   And watched how the stars grew high,
And the earth and skies were a splendid sight
   To a sober and musing eye.

From heaven the silver moon shone down,
   With a gentle and mellow ray,
And beneath, the crowded roofs of the town
   In broad light and shadow lay.

A glory was on the silent sea,
   And mainland and island too,
Till a haze came over the lowland lea,
   And shrouded the beautiful blue.

Bright in the moon the autumn wood
   Its crimson scarf unrolled,
And the trees like a splendid army stood,
   In a panoply of gold !

I saw them waving their banners high,
   As their crests to the night wind bowed;
And a distant sound on the air went by,
   Like the whispering of a crowd.

Then I watched from my windows how fast
   The lights around me fled,
As the wearied man to his slumber passed,
   And the sick one to his bed.

All faded save one; that burned
   With a distant and steady light;
But that, too, went out, and I turned
   When my own lamp within shone bright !

Thus, thought I, our joys must die;
  Yes, the brightest from earth we win;
Till each turns away, with a sigh,
  To the lamp that burns brightly within.

THE CITY AND THE SEA.

THE panting City cried to the Sea,
" I am faint with heat,—O breathe on me !

And the Sea said, "Lo, I breathe ! but my breath
To some will be life, to others death !"

As to Prometheus, bringing ease
In pain, come the Oceanides,

So to the City, hot with flame
Of the pitiless sun, the east wind came.

It came from the heaving breast of the deep,
Silent as dreams are, and sudden as sleep.

Life-giving, death-giving, which will it be,
O breath of the merciful, merciless Sea ?

LOSS AND GAIN.

WHEN I compare
What I have lost with what I have gained,
What I have missed with what attained,
  Little room do I find for pride.

I am aware
How many days have been idly spent ;
How like an arrow the good intent
  Has fallen short or been turned aside.

But who shall dare
To measure loss and gain in this wise?
Defeat may be victory in disguise;
The lowest ebb is the turn of the tide.

————◆————

CHARLES SUMNER.

GARLANDS upon his grave,
  And flowers upon his hearse,
And to the tender heart and brave
  The tribute of this verse.

His was the troubled life,
  The conflict and the pain,
The grief, the bitterness of strife,
  The honor without stain.

Death takes us by surprise,
  And stays our hurrying feet;
The great design unfinished lies,
  Our lives are incomplete.

But in the dark unknown
  Perfect their circles seem,
Even as a bridge's arch of stone
  Is rounded in the stream.

Were a star quenched on high,
  For ages would its light,
Still traveling downward from the sky,
  Shine on our mortal sight.

So when a great man dies,
  For years beyond our ken
The light he leaves behind him lies
  Upon the paths of men.

JAMES RUSSELL LOWELL.

Born Feb. 22, 1819.

JAMES RUSSELL LOWELL.

[HARVARD COMMENCEMENT POEM.]

OLIVER WENDELL HOLMES.

THIS is your month, the month of perfect days,
Birds in full song and blossoms all ablaze;
Nature herself your earliest welcome breathes,
Spreads every leaflet, every bower in wreaths;
Carpets her paths for your returning feet,
Puts forth her best your coming steps to greet;
And Heaven must surely find the earth in tune
When Home, sweet Home, exhales the breath of June.
These blessed days are waning all too fast,
And June's bright visions mingling with the past;
Lilacs have bloomed and faded, and the rose
Has dropped its petals, but the clover blows
And fills its slender tubes with honeyed sweets;
The fields are pearled with milk-white margarites;
The dandelion, which you sang of old,
Has lost its pride of place, its crown of gold,
But still displays its feathery-mantled globe,
Which children's breath or wandering winds unrobe.
These were your humble friends; your opened eyes
Nature had trained her common gifts to prize;
Not Cam or Isis taught you to despise
Charles, with his muddy margin, and the harsh,
Plebeian grasses of the reeking marsh.

New England's home-bred scholar, well you knew
Her soil, her speech, her people, through and through,
And loved them ever with the love that holds
All sweet, fond memories in its fragrant folds.
Though far and wide your winged words had flown,
Your daily presence kept you all our own,
Till with a sorrowing sigh, a thrill of pride,
We heard your summons, and you left our side
For larger duties and for tasks untried.

Atlantic Monthly.

———◆———

WE have been under the necessity of telling some unpleasant truths about American literature from time to time ; and it is with hearty pleasure that we are now able to own that the Britishers have been, for the present, utterly aud apparently hopelessly beaten by a Yankee in one important department of poetry. The tyranny of a vulgar public opinion and the charlatanism which is the price of political power, are butts for the shafts of the satirist which European poets may well envy Mr. Lowell.—*North British Review.*

———◆———

THOUGH eminent and able in many ways, Lowell remains absolutely a poet in feeling. His native genius was fostered by the associations of a singularly beautiful home ; nourished by the works of the dramatists, by the ideal pictures of poets and novelists, by the tender solemnity of the discourses of his father, and of Channing and others of his father's friends. Though he was not a rhyming prodigy like Pope, lisping in numbers, his first effusions as he came to manhood were in poetic form.—FRANCES H. UNDERWOOD.

LOWELL is a remarkable man and poet. That he is one of the first poets of this age, no man will deny. He is sincerely a reformer; his sympathies are entirely with the oppressed and down-trodden. Some of his poems are exceedingly beautiful, while others are full of grand thoughts which strike upon the ear and heart like the booming cannon-shot, which tells that an ardently desired conflict has commenced.—DAVID W. BARTLETT.

THE most characteristic and most essential happens to be the most salient quality of Mr. Lowell's style. It is a wit that is as omnipresent and as tireless as electricity itself. The effect is quite indescribable. We are sure that no other equal amount of literature could be produced that would yield to a competent assay a larger net result of pure wit. Generally the spirit of the wit is humane and gracious.—W. C. WILKINSON.

MR. LOWELL says somewhere that the art of writing consists largely in knowing what to leave in the ink-pot. How many volumes of Lowell's prose works if not in the waste-basket are almost as effectually buried in papers and magazines? What his working life has given to the world will give the reader some notion of what the world has not got, and will serve to call attention to the condensed wealth contained in "Among my Books" and "My Study Windows."—REV. H. R. HAWEIS.

A LOWELL ALPHABET.

ANOTHER star 'neath Time's horizon dropped
　To gleam o'er unknown lands and seas;
Another heart that beat for freedom stopped,—
　What mournful words are these !
　　　　　　　　　　To the Memory of Hood.

　Bowing then his head, he listened
　　For an answer to his prayer;
　No loud burst of thunder followed,
　　Not a murmur stirred the air.
　　　　　　　　　　　A Parable.

　Care, not of self, but of the common weal,
　Had robbed their eyes of youth, and left instead
　A look of patient power and iron will.
　　　　　　　A Glance behind the Curtain.

　Dear, common flower, that grow'st beside the way
　Fringing the dusty road with harmless gold,
　　First pledge of blithesome May.
　　　　　　　　　　To the Dandelion.

Each man is some man's servant; every soul
Is by some other's presence quite discrowned;
Each owes the next through all the imperfect round.
　　　　　　　　　　　The Pioneer.

　　For mankind are one in spirit,
　　　And an instinct bears along,
　　Round the earth's electric circle,
　　　The swift flash of right or wrong.
　　　　　　　　　　The Present Crisis.

　　　Glorious fountain !
　　　　Let my heart be
　　　Fresh, changeful, constant,
　　　　Upward, like thee !
　　　　　　　　　　The Fountain.

He could believe the promise of to-morrow
And feel the wondrous meaning of to-day;
He had a deeper faith in holy sorrow
Than the world's seeming loss could take away.

Ode.

It is God's day. It is Columbus's,
A lavish day ! One day, with life and heart,
Is more than time enough to find a world.

Columbus.

Joy comes, grief goes, we know not how;
Everything is happy now,
Everything is upward striving.

The Vision of Sir Launfal.

Knew you what silence was before ?
Here is no startle of dreaming bird
That sings in his sleep, or strives to sing.

Pictures from Appledore.

Life may be given in many ways,
And loyalty to Truth be sealed
As bravely in the closet as the field.

Commemoration Ode.

My soul went forth, and, mingling with the tree,
Danced in the leaves; or, floating in the cloud,
Saw its white double in the stream below.

Under the Willows.

Not always unimpeded can I pray,
Nor, pitying saint, thine intercession claim.

Sea-weed.

O realm of silence and of swart eclipse,
The shapes that haunt thy gloom
Make signs to us, and move thy withered lips
Across the gulf of doom.

To the Past.

Pan leaps and pipes all summer long,
The fairies dance each full-mooned night,
Would we but doff our lenses strong,
And trust our wiser eyes' delight.

The Foot-path.

Quite spent and out of breath he reached the tree,
And, listening fearfully, he heard once more
The low voice murmur "Rhoecus," close at hand.

Rhoecus.

Roots, wood, bark, and leaves singly perfect may be,
But, clapt hodge-podge together, they don't make a tree.

A Fable for Critics.

Since first I heard our North wind blow,
Since first I saw Atlantic throw
On our fierce rocks his thunderous snow,
I loved thee, Freedom!

Ode to France.

Thine is music such as yields
Feelings of old brooks and fields,
And, around this pent-up room,
Sheds a woodland, free perfume.

To Perdita, Singing.

Untremulous in the river clear,
Towards the sky's image, hangs the imaged bridge;
So still the air that I can hear
The slender clarion of the unseen midge.

Summer Storm.

Violet! sweet violet!
Thine eyes are full of tears;
Are they wet
Even yet
With the thought of other years?

Song.

Wrong ever builds on quicksands, but the Right
To the firm center lays its moveless base.

Prometheus.

Extemp'ry mammoth turkey-chick fer a Fejee Thanksgivin'.

The Biglow Papers.

Yet sets she not her soul so steadily
Above that she forgets her ties to earth.

Irene.

Zekle crep' up quite unbeknown
An' peeked in thru' the winder,
An' there sot Huldy all alone
'Ith no one nigh to hender.

The Courtin'.

———◆———

THE FIRST SNOW-FALL.

THE snow had begun in the gloaming,
And busily all the night
Had been heaping field and highway
With a silence deep and white.

Every pine and fir and hemlock
Wore ermine too dear for an earl,
And the poorest twig on the elm-tree
Was ridged inch deep with pearl.

From sheds new roof'd with Carrara
Came Chanticleer's muffled crow;
The stiff sails were softened to swan's down,
And still flutter'd down the snow.

I stood and watch'd by the window
The noiseless work of the sky,
And the sudden flurries of snow-birds
Like brown leaves whirling by.

I thought of a mound in sweet Auburn
　Where a little head-stone stood;
How the flakes were folding it gently,
　As did robins the babes in the wood.

Up spoke our own little Mabel,
　Saying, " Father, who makes it snow?"
And I told of the good All-father
　Who cares for us here below.

Again I look'd at the snow-fall,
　And thought of the leaden sky
That arch'd o'er our first great sorrow,
　When that mound was heap'd so high.

I remember'd the gradual patience
　That fell from that cloud like snow,
Flake by flake, healing and hiding
　The scar of our deep-plung'd woe.

And again to the child I whisper'd,
　" The snow that husheth all,
Darling, the merciful Father
　Alone can make it fall !"

Then, with eyes that saw not, I kiss'd her;
　And she, kissing back, could not know
That my kiss was given to her sister,
　Folded close under deepening snow.

ABRAHAM LINCOLN.

NATURE, they say, doth dote,
    And cannot make a man
    Save on some worn-out plan,
        Repeating us by rote.
For him her Old World molds aside she threw,
    And, choosing sweet clay from the breast
        Of the unexhausted West,
With stuff untainted shaped a hero new,
Wise, steadfast in the strength of God, and true.
        How beautiful to see
Once more a shepherd of mankind indeed,
Who loved his charge, but never loved to lead;
One whose meek flock the people joyed to be,
    Not lured by any cheat of birth,
    But by his clear-grained human worth,
And brave old wisdom of sincerity !
    They knew that outward grace is dust;
    They could not choose but trust
In that sure-footed mind's unfaltering skill,
        And supple-tempered will,
That bent like perfect steel to spring again and thrust.
    His was no lonely mountain-peak of mind—
    Broad prairie, rather, genial, level-lined,
    Fruitful and friendly for all human kind.
    Here was a type of the true elder race,
And one of Plutarch's men talked with us face to face.

* * *

WENDELL PHILLIPS.

HE stood upon the world's broad threshold ; wide
    The din of battle and of slaughter rolled;
He saw God stand upon the weaker side,
    That sank in seeming loss before its foes;
Many there were who made great haste and sold
    Unto the cunning enemy their swords.

He scorned their gifts of fame, and flower, and gold,
  And underneath their soft and flowery words
Heard the cold serpent hiss; therefore he went
  And humbly joined him to the weaker part.
Fanatic named, and fool, yet well content
  So he could be the nearer to God's heart,
And feel its solemn pulses sending blood
Through all the wide-spread veins of endless good.

FREEDOM.

MEN !—whose boast it is that ye
Come of fathers brave and free,
If there breathe on earth a slave,
Are ye truly free and brave?
If ye do not feel the chain
When it works a brother's pain,
Are ye not base slaves indeed—
Slaves unworthy to be freed?

Is true Freedom but to break
Fetters for our own dear sake,
And, with leathern hearts, forget
That we owe mankind a debt?
No !—true freedom is to share
All the chains our brothers wear,
And with heart and hand to be
Earnest to make others free !

They are slaves who fear to speak
For the fallen and the weak;
They are slaves who will not choose
Hatred, scoffing, and abuse,
Rather than in silence shrink
From the truth they needs must think.
They are slaves who dare not be
In the right with two or three.

JOHN GREENLEAF WHITTIER.
Born Dec. 17, 1807.

TO JOHN G. WHITTIER.

JAMES RUSSELL LOWELL.

NEW ENGLAND'S poet, rich in love as years,
  Her hills and valleys praise thee, and her brooks
  Dance to thy song; to her grave sylvan nooks
Thy feet allure us, which the wood-thrush hears
As maids their lovers, and no treason fears.
  Through thee her Merrimacks and Angloochooks,
  And many a name uncouth, win loving looks,
Sweetly familiar to both England's years.
Peaceful by birthright as a virgin lake
  The lily's anchorage which no eyes behold
Save those of stars, yet for thy brother's sake
  That lay in bonds, thou blew'st a blast as bold,
As that wherewith the heart of Roland brake
  Far heard through Pyrennean valleys cold.

IF there is any one in our age whom all men will ad-
mit to have been born a poet, it is Whittier. He is less
indebted to art, to scholastic culture, to the influences
of literary companionship, than any of his brethren.
He is a fiery apostle of human brotherhood, and has
chanted anathemas against war, and every form of cruel-
ty and superstition. He is eminently a national poet.
His mind is in full sympathy with the progressive ideas
of the New World.—FRANCES H. UNDERWOOD.

II

MUCH of Whittier's work has been in the form of contributions to journals which he has edited, and the two volumes which now constitute his collected prose writings have been gathered from these occasional papers. Himself of Quaker descent and belief, he has touched kindly but firmly the changing life of the day which culminated in the witchcraft delusion and displayed itself in the persecution of the Quakers. The carelessness of literary fame which Whittier has shown may be referred to the sincerity of his devotion to that which literature affects, and he has written and sung out of a heart very much in earnest to offer some help, or out of the pleasure of his work. The careful student of his writings will always value most the integrity of his life.—HORACE E. SCUDDER.

WHITTIER'S genius is Hebrew—more so than that of any other poet now using the English language. He is a flower of the moral sentiment in its masculine rigor, climbing like a forest pine. In this respect he affiliates with Wordsworth, and, going farther back, with Milton, whose tap-root was Hebrew. The man and the poet are one and the same.—REV. DAVID A. WASSON.

WHITTIER is in some respects the most American of all the American poets. It is safe to say that he has been less influenced by other literatures than any of our poets, with the exception, perhaps, of Bryant. The affectionate simplicity of Whittier's nature is seen in the poems which he addressed to his personal friends and to those whose life-pursuits ran in the same channels as his own moral sympathies.—RICHARD HENRY STODDARD.

I HAVE not seen John Greenleaf Whittier, but I have had correspondence with him and have great affection for him. During the American war an eminent citizen of Massachusetts told me he thought there was no man in the United States whose writings at that time, and for some years before then, had had such great influence on public opinion as the writings of Whittier. If God gives a real poet to the people at a time like that, does He not verily speak to the people and ask them to return to the ways of mercy and righteousness ?—JOHN BRIGHT.

A WHITTIER ALPHABET.

A COTTAGE hidden in the wood,
    Red through its seams a light is glowing,
On rock and bough and tree-trunk rude
    A narrow luster throwing.
                    Mogg Megone.

But welcome, be it old or new,
    The gift which makes the day more bright,
And paints upon the ground of cold
    And darkness warmth and light.
                    Flowers in Winter.

Cheerily then, my little man,
    Live and laugh as boyhood can !
Ah ! that thou couldst know thy joy
    Ere it passes, barefoot boy !
                    The Barefoot Boy.

Down on my native hills of June
    And home's green quiet, hiding all,
Fell sudden darkness like the fall
    Of midnight upon noon !
                    The Rendition.

Early hath the spoiler found thee,
   Brother of our love,
Autumn's faded earth around thee,
   And its storms above !
              On the Death of S. O. Torrey.

Father, to Thy suffering poor
   Strength and grace and faith impart,
And with Thy own love restore
   Comfort to the broken heart.
              The Familists' Hymn.

God's stars and silence taught thee
   As His angels only can,
That the one sole sacred thing beneath
   The cope of heaven is Man.
              The Branded Hand.

How hushed the hiss of party hate,
   The clamor of the throng !
How old, harsh voices of debate
   Flow into rhythmic song !
              My Birthday.

I walk, with noiseless feet, the round
   Of uneventful years;
Still o'er and o'er I sow the spring
   And reap the autumn ears.
              My Playmate.

Just then I felt the deacon's hand
   In wrath my coat-tail seize on;
I heard the priest cry, " Infidel !"
   The lawyer mutter, " Treason !"
              A Sabbath Scene.

Know we not our dead are looking
   Downward with a sad surprise,
All our strife of words rebuking
   With their mild and loving eyes ?
              A Visit to Washington.

Lift again the stately emblem
  On the Bay State's rusted shield;
Give to Northern winds the Pine Tree
  On our banner's tattered field.

The Pine Tree.

More than clouds of purple trail
  In the gold of setting day;
More than gleams of wing or sail
  Beckon from the sea-mist gray.

The Vanishers.

No perfect whole can our nature make,
  Here or there the circle will break;
The orb of life as it takes the light
  On one side, leaves the other in night.

The Preacher.

O friends whose hearts still keep their prime,
  Whose bright example warms and cheers,
Ye teach us how to smile at Time,
  And set to music all his years.

.The Laurels.

Proffering the riddles of the dread unknown
Like the calm Sphinxes, with their eyes of stone
Questioning the centuries from their veils of sand.

Trust.

Quiet and calm, without a fear
  Of danger darkly lurking near,
The weary laborer left his plow,
  The milkmaid caroled by her cow.

Pentucket.

Rivermouth Rocks are fair to see,
  By dawn or sunset shone across,
When the ebb of the sea has left them free
  To dry their fringes of gold-green moss.

The Wreck of Rivermouth.

So shall the Northern Pioneer go joyful on his way
To wed Penobscot's waters to San Francisco's bay.
The Crisis.

Thank God that I have lived to see the time
When the great truth begins at last to find
An utterance from the deep heart of mankind,
Earnest and clear, that all Revenge is Crime!
Abolition of the Gallows.

Unchanged by our changes of spirit and frame
Past, now, and henceforward the Lord is the same;
Though we sink in the darkness, His arms break our fall,
And in death as in life He is Father of all!
The Quaker Alumni.

Vain pride of star-lent genius!—vain
Quick fancy and creative brain,
Unblest by prayerful sacrifice,
Absurdly great or weakly wise!
The Chapel of the Hermits.

Wherever Freedom shivered a chain God speed, quoth I;
To Error amidst her shouting train I gave the lie.
My Soul and I.

Ximena, speak and tell us
Who has lost, and who has won?
Nearer came the storm and nearer,
Rolling fast and frightful on.
The Angels of Buena Vista.

Yon mountain's side is black with night,
While, broad-orbed, o'er its gleaming crown,
The moon, slow rounding into sight,
On the hushed, inland sea looks down.
Summer by the Lakeside.

Zephyr-like o'er all things going
When the breath divine is flowing,
All my yearnings to be free
Are as echoes answering Thee.
Hymn from the French.

THE MORAL WARFARE.

JOHN G. WHITTIER.

WHEN Freedom on her natal day
Within her war-rocked cradle lay,
An iron race around her stood,
Baptized her infant brow in blood;
And through the storm which round her swept
Their constant ward and watching kept.

Then, where our quiet herds repose
The roar of baleful battle rose,
And brethren of a common tongue
To mortal strife as tigers sprung;
And every gift on Freedom's shrine
Was man for beast, and blood for wine!

Our fathers to their graves have gone:
Their strife is past—their triumph won;
But sterner trials wait the race
Which rises in their honored place—
A moral warfare with the crime
And folly of an evil time.

So let it be. In God's own might
We gird us for the coming fight,
And, strong in Him whose cause is ours,
In conflict with unholy powers,
We grasp the weapon He has given—
The light, and truth, and love of heaven.

------◆------

RECENTLY a number of school-children of Girard, Pa.,
wrote a letter to John G. Whittier, the Quaker poet,
telling him that they had learned to recite "The Barefoot
Boy," "The Huskers," and "Maud Muller," and closing thus: "If it would not be too much trouble, please

write a verse for us—something that we could learn and always remember as having been written by you especially for us." In response he sent the following:

" Faint not and falter not, nor plead
Your weakness. Truth itself is strong;
The lion's strength, the eagle's speed,
Are not alone vouchsafed to wrong.

" Your nature, which, through fire and blood,
To place or gain can find its way,
Has power to seek the highest good,
And duty's holiest call obey."

MY COUNTRY.

LAND of the forest and the rock,
Of dark-blue lake and mighty river,
Of mountains reared aloft to mock
The storm's career, the lightning's shock;
My own green land forever !
O never may a son of thine,
Where'er his wandering steps incline,
Forget the skies which bent above
His childhood like a dream of love.

JOHN G. WHITTIER attended a reunion of his schoolmates at Haverhill, Mass., on the 10th of September, 1885. He was of the Class of '27. He wrote a poem for the occasion, which was read by a cousin of his. It is entitled "1827–1885," and is as follows:

The gulf of seven and fifty years
We stretch our welcoming hand across;
The distance but a pebble's toss
Between us and our youth appears.

For in life's school we linger on,
  The remnant of a once full list;
  Conning our lessons, undismissed,
With faces to the setting sun.

And some have gone the unknown way,
  And some await the call to rest;
  Who knoweth whether it is best
For those who went or us who stay?

And yet, despite of loss and ill,
  If faith and love and hope remain,
  Our length of days is not in vain,
And life is well worth living still.

Still to a gracious Providence
  The thanks of grateful hearts are due
  For blessings when our lives were new—
For all the good vouchsafed us since.

The pain that spared us sorer hurt;
  The wish denied, the purpose crossed;
  And pleasure, fond occasions lost,
These mercies to our small desert.

'Tis something that we wander back,
  Gray pilgrims, to the ancient ways,
  And tender memories of old days
Walk with us by the Merrimac.

That even in life's afternoon
  A sense of youth comes back again,
  As though this cool September rain
The still green woodlands dream of spring.

The eyes, grown dim to present things,
  Have keener sight for by-gone years,
  And sweet and clear in deafening ears
The bird that sang at morning sings.

Dear comrades, scattered wide and far
  Send from their homes their kindly word;
  And dearer ones, unseen, unheard,
Smile on us from some heavenly star.

For life and death with God are one;
  Unchanged by seeming change, His care
  And love are round us here and there;
He breaks no thread His hands have spun.

Soul touches soul; the muster-roll
  Of life eternal has no gaps;
  And after half a century's lapse
Our school-day ranks are closed and whole.

Hail and farewell! We go our way
  Where shadows end, we trust, in light;
  The star that ushers in the night
Is herald also of the day.

THE LIGHT THAT IS FELT.

A TENDER child of summers three,
  Seeking her little bed at night,
Paused on the dark stair timidly.
"O mother; take my hand," said she,
  "And then the dark will all be light."

We older children grope our way
  From dark behind to dark before;
And only when our hands we lay,
Dear Lord, in Thine, the night is day,
  And there is darkness nevermore.

Reach downward to the sunless days
  Wherein our guides are blind as we,
And faith is small and hope delays;
Take Thou the hands of prayer we raise,
  And let us feel the light of Thee.

DECORATION DAY.

HENRY WADSWORTH LONGFELLOW.

SLEEP, comrades, sleep and rest
　　On this Field of the Grounded Arms,
Where foes no more molest,
　　Nor sentry's shot alarms !

Ye have slept on the ground before,
　　And started to your feet
At the cannon's sudden roar,
　　Or the drum's redoubling beat.

But in this camp of Death
　　No sound your slumber breaks;
Here is no fevered breath—
　　No wound that bleeds and aches.

All is repose and peace;
　　Untrampled lies the sod;
The shouts of battle cease:
　　It is the Truce of God !

Rest, comrades, rest and sleep !
　　The thoughts of men shall be
As sentinels to keep
　　Your rest from danger free.

Your silent tents of green
　　We deck with fragrant flowers;
Yours has the suffering been,
　　The memory shall be ours.

BETWEEN THE GRAVES.

HARRIET PRESCOTT SPOFFORD.

WHERE blood once quenched the camp-fire's brand,
On every sod throughout the land
    The silver showers slip softly down;
On every sod some growing stem
    Lifts to the light a shining crown.

For underneath her bending blue,
With leaf and sunshine, moon and dew,
    Glad Nature gilds the graveside gloom,
Nor asks what passions stirred the dust
    Through which her pulses spring to bloom.

While from the gardens of the South,
Like blessings blown from some warm mouth,
    The wooing wind steals all day long—
Steals lingeringly from grave to grave,
    With breath of blossom, breath of song.

A common flag, breeze, showers and flowers,
Are weaving all these sunny hours,
    Where broken hearts and hopes are hid,
And the great mother on each bed
    Lays it, a fragrant coverlid.

You, who with garlands go about,
As the tree-tilting bird pours out
    O'er either mound his singing bliss,
Oh, kind as birds and breezes, leave
    A flower on that grave, and on this!

For, lo, the eternal truce of death
Was called upon the passing breath,
    And all the phantom hates, that shed
Their shadows round us as they stalked,
    Have no remembrance with the dead!

RED, WHITE, AND BLUE.

HARRIET MCEWEN KIMBALL.

RED Cypress ! unto him who grieves,
Reading sad legends in thy leaves,
    And finding in thy flower
An emblem of the heart that bleeds,
Say: The red blossom which I bear
        Doth symbolize
        The sacrifice
Of that sublimest hour
When Love fulfilled all human needs;
Bound Death, the Victor, as a slave;
Flung wide the sealed gates of the grave,
And set His angels, warders, there.

White Rose ! to him who gathers thee
The Flower of Consolation be—
    Unfolding peace, and not despair.
With sharpest thorns set round,
    Teach him how Life may wear
Sharp griefs, and yet be crowned !

Blue Harebell ! that dost tremble
    To the weird breath of Sorrow,
Be to the mourning one Faith's symbol;—
    Since thou dost borrow
    The same soft hue
Her eyes have won with constant looking up;
God filleth thine inverted cup
    With heaven's own blue;
So shall His sweet assurance fill
The heart bowed meekly to His will.

THE HEROES' DAY.

THROUGH the long bending grass
The white-robed maidens pass,
With tender faces, and with footsteps soft and slow,
Upon each lowly grave,
Where sleeps the true and brave,
Dropping red roses and wan lilies as they go.

Flowers for the patriot band
Who loved their native land:
Sweet rosemary, and purple pansies, and pale pinks;
Green leaves from budding trees
Make sweet the passing breeze—
Sweet as the elegy the grateful nation thinks.

For who would not prolong
With flowers and scent and song
The memory of those who fell in freedom's fight?
From the sweet month of May,
Then choose the fairest day,
And crown it for the honored dead with all things bright.

Then say: "O singing birds,
Echo these tender words:
While bosoms nobly throb, and women's eyes are wet,
While roses bud and blow,
While stars at evening glow,
While daylight breaks for us, we never will forget.

"As long as men shall stand
For home and native land,
And while our starry flag flies o'er the true and free,
Honor and love and truth
Shall give immortal youth,
And we'll remember you upon the land and sea."

Harper's Weekly.

DECORATION HYMN.

WILLIAM H. RANDALL.

SOLDIERS! who freely for our country's glory
    Upheld our flag on Southern hill and plain,
Long may your deeds be told in grateful story,
    Ye have not lived in vain!

Brothers! who fought for more than empty honor
    That all our land united might be free,
May shine for evermore upon our banner
    Each star for liberty.

Heroes! who toiled through all the dusty marches,
    And life surrendered on those shot-plowed fields,
To ye who fled where the blue sky o'erarches,
    Tribute a nation yields.

Your spirits, watching from out heaven's dominions,
    Shall not see lost what ye so dearly bought;
The shackles that once clogged the eagle's pinions
    Shall not again be wrought.

And now with garlands decorate each dwelling
    Where all that earth could claim serenely sleeps;
While love, like perfume from the flower upwelling
    Grateful remembrance keeps.

FLOWERS FOR THE BRAVE.

CELIA THAXTER.

HERE bring your purple and gold,
    Glory of color and scent!
Scarlet of tulips bold,
    Buds blue as the firmament.

Hushed is the sound of the fife
And the bugle piping clear:
The vivid and delicate life
In the soul of the youthful year.

We bring to the quiet dead,
With a gentle and tempered grief;
O'er the mounds so mute we shed
The beauty of blossoms and leaf.

The flashing swords that were drawn
No rust shall their fame destroy !
Boughs rosy as rifts of dawn,
Like the blush on the cheek of joy.

Rich fires of the gardens and meads,
We kindle these hearts above.
What splendor shall match their deeds;
What sweetness can match our love ?

----◆----

MEMORIAL DAY.

MARGARET SIDNEY.

A LITTLE window-garden plot,
Blooming in dusty street,
Adown which poured the travel
Of many weary feet;
A cheery spot of brightness
Blooming for all to see.
Oh, that was Blossom's garden-bed,
Who loved it tenderly.

At morn, at noon, at even,
She dealt out faithful care;
And many buds and flowerets sweet
Came out with fragrance rare.
And now, this May-day morning,
She stood in wealth of bloom
That beautified and perfumed all
The quaint, old-fashioned room.

When suddenly the door was thrown
  Ajar, and there stood Ray.
"Give us your flowers, do, Blossom, do,
  For Decoration Day."
She looked around with pretty flush
  Of hurt surprise: "Ah, no;
You know not what you ask, if you
  Would wish to rob me so."

"To *rob* you?" Master Ray in scorn
  Flashed out, then turned away;
"The soldiers gave their all for *you:*
  You *owe* them flowers to-day."
"I '*owe* them flowers.' Ah, true, indeed!
  Dear brother, please forgive.
Those brave men died on battle-fields
  That we at home might live;

And I not lay a flower upon
  Their graves in memory sweet!
Oh, selfish heart! I have to mourn
  Ingratitude complete.
Forgive me, Lord. They shall have all;
  Yes, glad I am to make
My buds and blossoms into wreaths
  For those dear patriots' sake."

The May-day sun shone brilliantly;
  All Nature smiled to see
The honors given to those who died
  In the cause of Liberty;
But the sweetest gift from loving hands
  Was the bud, and flower, and spray,
From the little child who gave her all
  On that Memorial Day.

12

THANKSGIVING.

THANKSGIVING DAY.

IT was not until the late civil war that this day became in any sense a National one. Until that time its observance was confined almost exclusively to New England. But the proclamation of President Johnson, Nov. 2, 1865, appointing a day for national thanksgiving, was indorsed by similar proclamations from the governors of all the States not of the late Confederacy, and since then the festival has steadily increased in popular favor, though many Southern States have been slow in its observance. Now that its appointment comes from a Democratic President,—the first one ever issued from such a source,—it is probable that it will be more generally regarded than ever before in our history. And this is one of the good signs of the times. It is well that one day of the year be given to the reunion of families, to the gathering together of scattered friends, and to rejoicing over the bounties of Providence.—*The Advance.*

THANKSGIVING AMONG THE GREEKS.

THE Greeks held the grandest feast of all the year in honor of Demeter, the goddess of the harvest; and the Romans, who borrowed most of their customs from the Grecians, also held a grand celebration in honor of the same goddess, whose name they changed to Ceres. They went in long processions to the fields, where they engaged in rustic sports, and crowned all of their household gods with flowers. Both of these feasts were held in September.

———◆———

THANKSGIVING AMONG THE JEWS.

THREE thousand years ago witnessed the Jewish Feast of Tabernacles, with its magnificent rituals, melodious choirs, and picturesque festivities. For eight days the people ceased their work, to "eat, drink, and be merry." During the time millions gathered in and around Jerusalem, for several days, living in booths formed of the branches of the olive, pine, myrtle, and palm, and decorated with fruits and flowers. Grand public pageants were held, and in addition to these every household had its worship, its sacrifice, and its banquet.

———◆———

THE FIRST ENGLISH THANKSGIVING IN NEW YORK.

BUT the Dutch went, and the English came—and they came to stay. On the possession of New Netherland by the English, Edmund Andros being Governor, the Council sitting on June 7, 1675, ordered :

"That Wednesday ye 23d of this Instant month, be appointed throughout ye government a day of Thanksgiving and Prayers to Almighty God for all His Past Deliverances and Blessings and Present Mercies to us, and to Pray ye continuance and Encrease thereof."

How the Pilgrims gave Thanks.

The Pilgrim Fathers, after ten months of sickness and suffering, gathered in their first harvest, which consisted of twenty acres of corn, and six of barley and peas —enough to keep them supplied with food for the coming year. For this they devoutly thanked God, and made preparations for a feast. Hunters were sent out to procure the thanksgiving dinner, and returned with waterfowl, wild turkey, and venison. Then the feast was prepared, and Massasoit and ninety of his warriors were present. On the following year there was such a long drought that the corn and barley were stunted, and famine seemed to stare them in the face. A day of fasting and prayer was appointed, and for nine hours the people prayed unceasingly. At evening the sun set in clouds, a breeze sprang up, and in the morning the rain was pouring down. The crops revived, and there was a bounteous harvest. For this a day of thanksgiving was ordered by Governor Bradford.

The history of this first thanksgiving is recorded as follows:

"Our harvest being gotten in, our governor sent four men out a-fowling that we might, after a special manner, rejoice together after we had the fruit of our labor. They four, in one day, killed as much fowl as, with a little help beside, served the company almost a week. At that time, among other recreations, we exercised our arms, many of the Indians coming among us, and among the rest, their greatest king, Massasoit, with some ninety men, whom for three days we entertained and feasted, and they went out and killed five deer, which they brought to the plantation and bestowed on our governor and upon the captain and others. And although it be not always so plentiful as it was at this time with us, yet by the goodness of God we are so far from want that we often wish you partakers of our plenty."

THE FIRST NATIONAL THANKSGIVING.

THE immediate occasion of the first thanksgiving was the surrender of General Burgoyne to General Gates, in the fall of 1777. Thursday, the 18th of December, was designated, and, in compliance with the order of Congress, the army at Valley Forge duly observed the day—the army that had tracked its way in blood. It was ordered by the Continental Congress.

WASHINGTON'S PROCLAMATION.

WASHINGTON, as President of the United States, issued his first proclamation for the observance of a day of thanksgiving at the city of New York on the 3d of October, 1789, setting apart Thursday, the 26th day of November of that year, "to be devoted by the people of these States to the service of that great and glorious Being who is the beneficent Author of all the good that was, that is, or that will be," etc. His second proclamation, dated at the city of Philadelphia, January 1, 1795, designated Thursday, November 26, as a day to be observed for a general thanksgiving by the people of the United States.

Governor John Jay, of New York, thought so well of Thanksgiving Day, that he determined to have one of his own, and accordingly designated Thursday, November 26, 1795.

THE FIRST BOSTON THANKSGIVING—July, 1630.

[*For Concert and Solo Recitation.*]

HEZEKIAH BUTTERWORTH.

Solo. " PRAISE ye the Lord !"   The psalm to-day
    That rises on our ears
    Rolls from the hills of Boston Bay
    Through five times fifty years—
    When Winthrop's fleet from Yarmouth crept
    Out to the open main,
    And through the widening waters swept
    In April sun and rain,
Concert.   "Pray to the Lord with fervent lips,"
    The leader shouted, "pray;'
    And prayer arose from all the ships,
    As fadeth Yarmouth Bay.

Solo.   They passed the Scilly Isles that day,
    And May days came, and June,
    And thrice upon the ocean lay
    The full orb of the moon.
    And as that day, on Yarmouth Bay,
    Ere England sunk from view,
    While yet the rippling Solent lay
    In April skies of blue,
Concert.   "Pray to the Lord with fervent lips,"
    Each morn was shouted, "pray;"
    And prayer arose from all the ships,
    As first in Yarmouth Bay.

Solo.   Blew warm the breeze o'er Western seas,
    Through Maytime morns and June,
    Till hailed these souls the Isles of Shoals,
    Low, 'neath the summer moon;
    And as Cape Ann arose to view,
    And Norman's Woe they passed,
    The wood-doves came the white mist through
    And circled round each mast.

Concert.   "Pray to the Lord with fervent lips,"
Then called the leader, "pray;"
And prayer arose from all the ships,
As first in Yarmouth Bay.

Solo.   The white wings folded, anchors down,
The sea-worn fleet in line;
Fair rose the hills where Boston town
Should rise from clouds of pine;
Fair was the harbor, summit-walled,
And placid lay the sea.
"Praise ye the Lord," the leader called;
"Praise ye the Lord," spake he.
Concert.   "Give thanks to God with fervent lips,
Give thanks to God to-day."
The anthem rose from all the ships,
Safe moored in Boston Bay.

Solo.   That psalm our fathers sung we sing,
That psalm of peace and wars,
While o'er our heads unfolds its wing,
The flag of forty stars ;
And while the nation finds a tongue
For nobler gifts to pray,
'Twill ever sing the song they sung
That first Thanksgiving Day:
Concert.   "Praise ye the Lord with fervent lips,
Praise ye the Lord to-day."
So rose the song from all the ships,
Safe moored in Boston Bay.

Concert. Ho ! vanished ships from Yarmouth's tide,
Ho ! ships of Boston Bay,
Your prayers have crossed the centuries wide
To this Thanksgiving Day !
We pray to God with fervent lips,
We praise the Lord to-day,
As prayers arose from Yarmouth ships,
But psalms from Boston Bay.

THANKSGIVING FOR HIS HOUSE.

ROBERT HERRICK (1591–1674).

LORD, thou hast given me a cell
    Wherein to dwell,
A little house whose humble roof
    Is weather-proof;
Under the sparres of which I lie
    Both soft and dry;
Where thou, my chamber for to ward,
    Hast set a guard
Of harmless thoughts to watch and keep
    Me, while I sleep.
Low is my porch, as is my fate,
    Both void of state;
And yet the threshold of my doore
    Is worn by th' poore,
Who hither come, and freely get
    Good words, or meat.

'Tis thou that crownest my glittering hearth
    With guiltlesse mirthe,
And givest me wassaile bowls to drink,
    Spiced to the brink.
Lord, 'tis thy plenty-dropping hand
    That soiles my land
And givest me for my bushel sown
    Twice ten for one;
Thou makest my teeming hen to lay
    Her egg each day.
All these, and better, thou dost send
    Me, to this end,
That I should render, for my part,
    A thankful heart;
Which, fired with incense, I resigne
    As wholly Thine:
But the acceptance, that must be,
    O Lord, by Thee.

THANKSGIVING.

WILLIAM D. HOWELLS.

LORD, for the erring thought
Not into evil wrought!
Lord, for the wicked will
Betrayed and baffled still!
For the heart from itself kept,
Our thanksgiving accept.
For ignorant hopes that were
Broken to our blind prayer;
For pain, death, sorrow, sent
Unto our chastisement;
For all loss of seeming good,
Quicken our gratitude.

Harper's Magazine.

THANKSGIVING ODE.

JOHN G. WHITTIER.

ONCE more the liberal year laughs out
O'er richer stores than gems or gold;
Once more with harvest-song and shout
Is nature's bloodless triumph told.

Our common mother rests and sings,
Like Ruth, among her garnered sheaves;
Her lap is full of goodly things,
Her brow is bright with autumn leaves.

O favors every year made new!
O gifts with rain and sunshine sent!
The bounty overruns our due;
The fullness shames our discontent.

We shut our eyes, and flowers bloom on;
We murmur, but the corn-ears fill;
We choose the shadow, but the sun
That casts it shines behind us still.

God gives us with our rugged soil
    The power to make it Eden-fair,
And richer fruits to crown our toil
    Than summer-wedded islands bear.

Who murmurs at his lot to-day ?
    Who scorns his native fruit and bloom ?
Or sighs for dainties far away,
    Beside the bounteous board of home ?

Thank Heaven, instead, that Freedom's arm
    Can change a rocky soil to gold;
That brave and generous lives can warm
    A clime with Northern ices cold.

And let these altars, wreathed with flowers
    And piled with fruits, awake again
Thanksgivings for the golden hours,
    The early and the latter rain !

ELSIE'S THANKSGIVING.

MARGARET E. SANGSTER.

DOLLY, it's almost Thanksgiving; do you know what that
    means, my dear ?
No ? Well, I couldn't expect it; you haven't been with us a year,
And you came with my auntie from Paris, far over the wide
    blue sea,
And you'll keep your first Thanksgiving, my beautiful Dolly,
    with me.

I'll tell you about it, my darling, for grandma's explained it all,
So that I understand why Thanksgiving always comes late in
    the fall,
When the nuts and the apples are gathered, and the work in
    the field is done,
And the fields, all reaped and silent, are asleep in the autumn
    sun.

It is then that we praise Our Father who sends the rain and
the dew,
Whose wonderful loving-kindness is every morning new;
Unless we'd be heathen, Dolly, or worse, we must sing and
pray,
And think about good things, Dolly, when we keep Thanksgiving Day.

But I like it very much better when from church we all go
home,
And the married brothers and sisters and the troops of cousins
come,
And we're ever so long at the table, and dance and shout and
play,
In the merry evening, Dolly, that ends Thanksgiving day.

THANKSGIVINGS OF OLD.

E. A. SMULLER.

OH, the glorious Thanksgivings
Of the days that are no more!
How, with each recurring season,
Wakes their mem'ry o'er and o'er!
When the hearts of men were simpler,
And the needs of life were less,
And its mercies were not reckoned
By the measure of excess.

Heaven send the glad Thanksgiving
Of that older, simpler time!
Tarry with us, not in fancy,
Not in retrospective rhyme;
But in true and living earnest
May the spirit of that day,
Artless, plain, and unpretending,
Once again resume its sway!

CHRISTMAS.

THE DAY OF DAYS.

Solo. 'TWAS eighteen hundred years ago,
Not in a region of ice and snow,
But far in the land of the early morn,
The oldest of lands, our Christ was born.

Concert. Of all the joy-days under the sun,
Of all the holidays, there's but one
That comes to the heart, and clings to the home—
Christmas has come !

Solo. Still through the length of the multiplied years,
Sunshine of pleasure, and rainfall of tears,
Changes and growth in wonderful ways,
Christmas remains the great day of days.

Concert. The day of the hope that casteth out fear,
The day of all days that brings good cheer
In the country's peace and the city's hum—
Christmas has come !

Solo. Now in the uttermost ends of the earth
The story is told of the Christ-child's birth;
And millions, wherever the sun's rays fall,
Are kin in the hope that is dear to all.

Concert. All over the lands and far out on the seas
Is a lifting of voices and bowing of knees;
And alike to us all, if we rest or roam,
Christmas has come !

Solo. Wherever the blessings of mortals increase,
With customs and laws that give joy and peace;
Where science and art yield comfort and bliss,
All over the world there is no day like this.

Concert. Of all the joy-days under the sun,
Of all the holidays, there's but one
That touches the heart and clings to the home—
Christmas has come!

CHRISTMAS IN OLDEN TIME.

SIR WALTER SCOTT.

HEAP on more wood!—the wind is chill;
But, let it whistle as it will,
We'll keep our Christmas merry still.
Each age has deemed the new-born year
The fittest time for festal cheer.
And well our Christmas sires of old
Loved, when the year its course had rolled
And brought blithe Christmas back again
With all its hospitable train,
With social and religious rite
To honor all the holy night.
On Christmas-eve the bells were rung;
On Christmas-eve the mass was sung.
Then opened wide the Baron's hall
To vassal, tenant, serf, and all;
Power laid his rod of rule aside,
And Ceremony doffed her pride.
All hailed with uncontrolled delight
And general voice the happy night,
That to the cottage, as the crown,
Brought tidings of salvation down.
The fire, with well-dried logs supplied,
Went roaring up the chimney wide;

The huge hall-table's oaken face,
Scrubbed till it shone, the day to grace,
Bore then upon its massive board
No mark to part the squire and lord.
　Then came the merry maskers in
And carols roared with blithesome din.
If unmelodious was the song,
It was a hearty note and strong.
England was merry England when
Old Christmas brought his sports again.
'Twas Christmas broached the mightiest ale;
'Twas Christmas told the merriest tale;
A Christmas gambol oft could cheer
The poor man's heart through half the year.

A CHRISTMAS THOUGHT ABOUT DICKENS.

BERTHA S. SCRANTON.

WESTMINSTER is gray at midnight,
　With shadows from wall to wall;
They have noiseless feet, these shadows,
　And make no sound as they fall.
But I ween they will creep together,
　A goodly band to-night,
Over a silent marble name,
　In the Christmas-eve twilight.

All the tiny dear child-people
　We hold in our hearts to-day,
Who will live when that same marble
　Has crumbled to dust away.
"Little Em'ly's" ghost that haunteth
　The minster's shadowy aisle,
With the grave, sweet face of Agnes,
　And the child-wife Dora's smile.

Then will come, I ween, with the others,
  Poor Smike with his patient air,
And the seven little Kenwigs,
  With their braided tails of hair.
And Jenny Wren, I can promise,
  Will surely be there again,
With her slanting rows of children,
  Crying, " Who is this in pain ?"

Little Nell will wake and listen,
  When the white, white world is still
And the great chimes through the midnight
  From the belfry tower thrill.
The little Cratchits will hearken
  And wait till the goose is done,
And the voice of tiny Tim will cry,
  " God bless us every one !"

But ah ! for the living mourners
  On either side of the sea,
For whom no more the brave hand writes,
  The heart beats cheerily.
And ah ! for the saddened chambers,
  Where his watchers ever wait,
They unto whom life yields but pain,
  And who keep its vigil late.

Westminster is gray with shadows,
  But his children never die !
Through all the Christmas times to come
  Will his carol notes ring high.
The dreamer has but awakened,
  And the master's work is done,
But the bells on Time's great steeple
  Ring, " God bless us every one !"

[In the following selection the numbered stanzas can be given in concert with a musical accompaniment.]

THE STAR IN THE WEST.

QUEBEC—1635.

HEZEKIAH BUTTERWORTH.

'TIS the fortress of St. Louis,
  The Church of Recoverance,
And hang o'er the crystal crosses
  The silver lilies of France.
In the fortress a knight lies dying,
  In the church are priests at prayer,
And the bell of the Angelus sweetly
  Throbs out on the crimsoned air.

The noblest knight is dying
  That ever served a king,
And he looks from the fortress window
  As the bells of the Angelus ring.
Old scenes come back to his vision,
  Again his ship's canvases swell
In the harbor of gray St. Malo,
  In the haven of fair Rochelle.
He sees the emparadised ocean
  That he dared when his years were young,
The lagoons where his lateen-sail drifted
  As the Southern Cross over it hung;
Acadie, the Richelieu's waters,
  The lakes through the midlands that rolled,
And the cross that he planted wherever
  He lifted the lilies of gold.
He lists to the Angelus ringing,
  He folds his white hands on his breast,
And far o'er the clouded forests
  A star verges low in the West !

I.

" Star on the bosom of the West,
    Chime on, O bell, chime on, O bell !
To-night with visions I am blest,
    And filled with light ineffable !
No angels sing in crystal air,
    No clouds 'neath seraphs' footsteps glow,
No feet of seers o'er mountains fair
    A portent follows far; but lo !
    A star is glowing in the West,
        The world shall follow it from far—
    Chime on, O Christmas bells, chime on !
    Shine on, shine on, O Western Star !

II.

. " In yonder church that storms have iced—
    I founded it upon this rock—
I've daily kissed the feet of Christ,
    In worship with my little flock.
But I am dying—I depart,
    Like Simeon old my glad feet go,
A star is shining in my heart.
    Such as the Magi saw; and lo !
    A star is shining in the West,
        The world shall hail it from afar !
    Chime on, O Christmas bells, chime on !
    Shine on, shine on, O Western Star !

III.

" Beside the Fleur de Lis of France,
    The faith I've planted in the North,
Ye messengers of Heaven, advance;
    Ye mysteries of the Cross, shine forth !
I know the value of the earth,
    I've learned its lessons; it is done;
One soul alone outweighs in worth
    The fairest kingdom of the sun.

13

Star on the bosom of the West,
My dim eyes follow thee afar.
Chime on, chime on, O Christmas bells!
Shine on, shine on, O golden Star!

IV.

"What rapture! hear the sweet choirs sing,
While death's cold shadows o'er me fall,
Beneath the lilies of my King—
Go, light the lamps in yonder hall.
Mine eyes have seen the Christ Star glow
Above the New World's temple gates.
. Go forth, celestial heralds, go!
Earth's fairest empire thee awaits!
Star on the bosom of the West,
What feet shall follow thee from far?
Chime on, O Christmas bells, chime on!
Shine on forever, golden Star!"

'Twas Christmas morn; the sun arose
'Mid clouds o'er the St. Lawrence broad,
And fell a sprinkling of the snows
As from the uplifted hand of God.
Dead in the fortress lay the knight,
His white hands crossed upon his breast,
Dead, he whose clear prophetic sight
Beheld the Christ Star in the West.
That morning, 'mid the turrets white,
The low flags told the empire's last,
They hung the lilies o'er the knight,
And by the lilies set the cross.

. Long, on Quebec, immortal heights,
Has Champlain slept, the knight of God;
The Western Star shines on, and lights
The growing empire, fair and broad.
And though are gone the knights of France,
Still lives the spirit of the North;
The heralds of the Star advance,
And Truth's eternal light shines forth.

THE LITTLE MUD-SPARROWS.

(*A Jewish Legend.*)

ELIZABETH STUART PHELPS.

I LIKE that old sweet legend
    Not found in Holy Writ,
And wish that John or Matthew
    Had made Bible out of it.

But though it is not Gospel,
    There is no law to hold
The heart from growing better
    That hears the story told:

How the little Jewish children
    Upon a summer day
Went down across the meadows
    With the Child Christ to play,

And in the gold-green valley
    Where low the reed-grass lay,
They made them mock mud-sparrows
    Out of the meadow-clay.

So, when these all were fashioned
    And ranged in flocks about,
" Now," said the little Jesus,
    " We'll let the birds fly out."

Then all the happy children
    Did call, and coax, and cry—
Each to his own mud-sparrow:
    " Fly, as I bid you—fly !"

But earthen were the sparrows,
    And earth they did remain,
Though loud the Jewish children
    Cried out and cried again—

Except the one bird only
    The little Lord Christ made.
The earth that owned Him Master,
    —His earth heard and obeyed.

Softly He leaned and whispered:
    " Fly up to heaven ! fly !"
And swift His little sparrow
    Went soaring to the sky.

And silent all the children
    Stood awe-struck looking on,
Till deep into the heavens
    The bird of earth had gone.

I like to think for playmate
    We have the Lord Christ still,
And that still above our weakness,
    He works His mighty will;

That all our little playthings
    Of earthen hopes and joys
Shall be by His commandment
    Changed into heavenly toys.

Our souls are like the sparrows
    Imprisoned in the clay—
Bless Him who came to give them wings,
    Upon a Christmas Day !

A Christmas Question.

Rev. Minot J. Savage.

[For concert recitation. In order to avoid monotony in the repetition of the question, the first line of the first stanza can be read with direct falling slides; of the second, with direct rising slides; of the third, with emphasis on the first word; of the fourth, with a perfect monotone; of the fifth, with emphasis on the second word; of the sixth, with direct rising slides.]

I.

When will He come?
A captive nation dwell upon
The river-banks of Babylon;
What is the word they speak?
The prophet's eye looks down the years
And kindles as the sight appears—
"Messiah! him ye seek!
Lo! the Lord's anointed comes! and then
Shall dwell the heavenly kingdom among men!"

II.

When will He come?
The Christian answers, "Long ago
The King was born in manger low.
Him wicked men have slain,
And now we wait with longing eye,
And fix our look upon the sky;
For He will come again,
We pray and watch since He has gone away;
For when He comes He'll bring the perfect day."

III.

When will He come?
"Lo, here! Lo, there!" the foolish shout,
And think that God will come without.
But ever has it been,
In spite of fabled tales that tell

Of magic and of miracle,
That He has come within.
Only through man, and man alone,
Does God build up his righteous throne.

IV.

When will He come?
When iron first was hammered out;
When far shores heard the seaman's shout;
When letters first were known;
When separate tribes to nations grew;
When men their brotherhood first knew;
When law first reached the throne:
Each separate upward step that man has trod
Has been a coming of the living God.

V.

When will He come?
While you are looking far away,
His tireless feet are nigh to-day;
Each true word is His voice.
All honest work, all noble trust,
Each deed that lifts man from the dust,
Each pure and manly choice,
Each upward stair man's toil-worn feet do climb,
Is just another birth of God sublime.

VI.

When will He come?
He'll come to-morrow if you will;
But cease your idle sitting still.
Yes, He will come to-day.
He will not come in clouds; but through
Your doing all that you can do
To help the right alway.
Do honest work, and to the truth be true,
And God already has appeared in you.

WINGS.

DINAH MULOCK CRAIK.

"MOTHER, oh, make me a pair of wings,
　　Like the Christ-child's adorning;
Blue as the sky, with a gold star-eye—
　　I'll wear them on Christmas morning."

The mother worked with a careless heart
　　All through that merry morning;
Happy and blind, nor saw behind
　　The shadow that gives no warning.

He struck—and over the little face
　　A sudden change came creeping;
Twelve struggling hours against Death's fierce powers,
　　And then—he has left her sleeping.

Strange sleep that no mother's kiss can wake !
　　Lay her pretty wings beside her;
Strew white flowers sweet on her hands and feet,
　　And under the white snow hide her.

For the Christ-child called her out of her play,
　　And, thus our earth-life scorning,
She went away.　What, dead, we say ?
　　She was born that Christmas morning.
　　　　　　　　　　　　　　　Wide Awake.

THE NATIVITY.

LOUISA PARSONS HOPKINS.

FROM Nazareth to Bethlehem,
Their holy journey leading them
By silver-towered Jerusalem.

Beneath the palm-tree's tossing plume,
Amid the harvest's rich perfume,
No house could give them rest or room.

So entering at the wayside cave,
Where mountain-rills the limestone lave,
The child was born a world to save.

They laid him in the manger white;
The lowing oxen saw the sight,
And wondered at the dazzling light.

The mother's heart in sacred bliss
Could dream no sweeter heaven than this,
To greet her babe with mother's kiss.

And bending down with sacred awe,
For a lost world the angels saw
Love, the fulfilling of the law.

A CHRISTMAS day, to be perfect, should be clear and
cold, with holly branches in berry, a blazing fire, a dinner with mince-pies, and games and forfeits in the evening. You cannot have it in perfection if you are very
fine and fashionable. A Christmas evening should, if
possible, finish with music. It carries off the excite-
ment without abruptness, and sheds a repose over the
conclusion of enjoyment.—LEIGH HUNT.

CHRISTMAS BELLS.

HENRY WADSWORTH LONGFELLOW.

[For musical accompaniment]

I HEARD the bells on Christmas-day
Their old, familiar carols play,
    And wild and sweet
    The words repeat
Of peace on earth, good-will to men !

And thought how, as the day had come,
The belfries of all Christendom
    Had rolled along
    The unbroken song
Of peace on earth, good-will to men !

Till, ringing, swinging on its way,
The world revolved from night to day
    A voice, a chime,
    A chant sublime
Of peace on earth, good-will to men !

Then from each black, accursèd mouth
The cannon thundered in the South
    And with the sound
    The carols drowned
Of peace on earth, good-will to men !

It was as if an earthquake rent
The hearth-stones of a continent,
    And made forlorn
    The households born
Of peace on earth, good-will to men !

And in despair I bowed my head;
"There is no peace on earth," I said;
    "For hate is strong
    And mocks the song
Of peace on earth, good-will to men !"

Then pealed the bells more loud and deep;
"God is not dead; nor doth he sleep !
    The Wrong shall fail,
    The Right prevail,
With peace on earth, good-will to men !"

CHRISTMAS ROSES.

MAY RILEY SMITH.

I GAVE into a brown and tirèd hand
A stem of roses, sweet and creamy-white.
I know the bells rang merry tunes that night,
For it was Christmas time throughout the land,
And all the skies were hung with lanterns bright.

The brown hand held my roses gracelessly;
They seemed more white within their dusky vase;
A scarlet wave suffused the woman's face.
"My hands so seldom hold a flower," said she,
"I think the lovely things feel out of place."

O tirèd hands that are unused to flowers;
O feet that tread on nettles all the way !
God grant His peace may fold you round to-day,
And cling in fragrance when these Christmas hours,
With all their mirthfulness, have passed away !

NEW-YEAR'S.

ADDRESS TO THE NEW YEAR.

DINAH MULOCK CRAIK.

O GOOD New Year ! we clasp
  This warm, shut hand of thine,
Loosing forever, with half sigh, half grasp,
  That which from ours falls like dead fingers' twine.
Ay, whether fierce its grasp
Has been, or gentle, having been, we know
That it was blessed: let the old year go.

Friend, come thou like a friend;
  And, whether bright thy face,
Or dim with clouds we cannot comprehend,
  We'll hold our patient hands, each in his place,
And trust thee to the end,
Knowing thou leadest onwards to those spheres
Where there are neither days nor months nor years.

A NEW YEAR.

MARGARET E. SANGSTER.

WHY do we greet thee, O blithe New Year !
What are thy pledges of mirth and cheer ?
Comest, knight-errant, the wrong to right ?
Comest to scatter our gloom with light ?
Wherefore the thrill, the sparkle and shine,
In heart and eyes at a word of thine ?

The old was buoyant, the old was true,
The old was brave when the old was new.
He crowned us often with grace and gift;
His sternest skies had a deep blue rift.
Straight and swift, when his hand unclasped,
With welcome and joyance thine we grasped.
O tell us, Year—we are fain to know—
What is thy charm that we hail thee so?

Dost promise much that is fair and sweet—
The wind's low stir in the rippling wheat,
The waves' soft plash on the sandy floor,
The bloom of roses from shore to shore,
Glance of wings from the bowery nest,
Music and perfume from east to west,
Frosts to glitter in jeweled rime,
Blush of sunrise at morning's prime,
Stars above us their watch to keep,
And rain and dew, though we wake or sleep?

Once more a voice, and I hear it call
Like a bugle-note from a mountain wall;
The pines uplift it with mighty sound,
The billows bear it the green earth round;
A voice that rolls in a jubilant song,
A conqueror's ring in its echo strong;
Through the ether clear, from the solemn sky
The New Year beckons, and makes reply:

"I bring you, friends, what the years have brought
Since ever men toiled, aspired, or thought—
Days for labor, and nights for rest;
And I bring you love, a heaven-born guest;
Space to work in, and work to do,
And faith in that which is pure and true.
Hold me in honor and greet me dear,
And sooth you'll find me a Happy Year."

Harper's Bazar.

A WISH.

MARGARET VELEY.

IF I could find the Little Year,
The Happy Year, the glad New Year—
If I could find him setting forth
To seek the ancient track—
I'd bring him here, the Little Year,
Like a peddler with his pack.

And all of golden brightness,
And nothing dull or black,
And all that heart could fancy,
And all that life could lack,
Should be your share of the peddler's ware,
When he undid his pack.

The best from out his treasure
A smile of yours would coax,
And then we'd speed him on his way,
At midnight's failing strokes;
And bid him hurry round the world,
And serve the other folks !

ANOTHER YEAR.

NATHANIEL P. WILLIS.

SWEETLY hath passed the year; the seasons came
Duly as they were wont, the gentle spring,
And the delicious summer, and the cool,
Rich autumn, with the nodding of the grain,
And winter, like an old and hoary man,
Frosty and stiff—and so are chronicled.

We have read gladness in the new green leaf,
And in the first-blown violets; we have drunk
Cool water from the rock, and in the shade
Sunk to the noontide slumber; we have plucked
The mellow fruitage of the bending tree,
And girded to our pleasant wanderings.

When the cool winds came freshly from the hills,
And when the tinting of the autumn leaves
Had faded from its glory, we have sat
By the good fires of winter, and rejoiced
Over the fullness of the gathered sheaf.

THE CHILD AND THE YEAR.

CELIA THAXTER.

SAID the child to the youthful year:
" What hast thou in store for me,
O giver of beautiful gifts ! what cheer,
What joy dost thou bring with thee ?"

" My seasons four shall bring
Their treasures: the winter's snows,
The autumn's store, and the flowers of spring,
And the summer's perfect rose.

" All these and more shall be thine,
Dear child,—but the last and best
Thyself must earn by a strife divine,
If thou wouldst be truly blest.

" Wouldst know this last, best gift?
'Tis a conscience clear and bright,
A peace of mind which the soul can lift
To an infinite delight.

" Truth, patience, courage, and love,
If thou unto me canst bring,
I will set thee all earth's ills above,
O child ! and crown thee a king !"

WE are bound, by every rule of justice and equity, to give the New Year credit for being a good one until he proves himself unworthy the confidence we repose in him.—CHARLES DICKENS.

THE SEASONS.

A SONG OF WAKING.

KATHARINE LEE BATES.

THE maple buds are red, are red,
  The robin's call is sweet;
The blue sky floats above thy head,
  The violets kiss thy feet.
The sun paints emeralds on the spray
  And sapphires on the lake;
A million wings unfold to-day,
  A million flowers awake.

Their starry cups the cowslips lift
  To catch the golden light,
And like a spirit fresh from shrift
  The cherry tree is white.
The innocent looks up with eyes
  That know no deeper shade
Than falls from wings of butterflies
  Too fair to make afraid.

With long, green raiment blown and wet
  The willows, hand in hand,
Lean low to teach the rivulet
  What trees may understand
Of murmurous tune and idle dance,
  With broken rhymes whose flow
A poet's ear shall catch, perchance,
  A score of miles below.

Across the sky to fairy realm
  There sails a cloud-born ship;
A wind sprite standeth at the helm,
  With laughter on his lip;

The melting masts are tipped with gold,
　The 'broidered pennons stream;
The vessel beareth in her hold
　The lading of a dream.

It is the hour to rend thy chains,
　The blossom time of souls;
Yield all the rest to cares and pains,
　To-day delight controls.
Gird on thy glory and thy pride,
　For growth is of the sun;
Expand thy wings whate'er betide,
　The Summer is begun.

———◆———

"Early Spring."

Alfred Tennyson.

I.

Once more the Heavenly Power
　Makes all things new,
And domes the red-plowed hills
　With loving blue;
The blackbirds have their wills,
　The throstles too.

II.

Opens a door in Heaven
　From skies of glass;
A Jacob's-ladder falls
　On greening grass,
And o'er the mountain-walls
　Young angels pass.

III.

Before them fleets the shower,
　And burst the buds,
And shine the level lands,

And flash the floods;
The stars are from their hands
Flung through the woods.

IV.

O follow, leaping blood,
The season's lure !
O heart, look down and up,
Serene, secure,
Warm as the crocus-cup,
Like snow-drops, pure !

V.

For now the Heavenly Power
Makes all things new,
And thaws the cold and fills
The flower with dew;
The blackbirds have their wills,
The poets too.

Youth's Companion.

MAY.

MAY comes laughing, crowned with daffodils,
    Her dress embroidered with blue violets,
    So gracious and so sweet she scarcely lets
A thought return of all the winter's ills.
The orchards with enchanting wealth she fills;
    In the green marshes golden cowslip sets,
    And all the waking woodland spaces frets
With shy anemones.   But ah, she wills
At times to frown in sudden wayward mood;
    The violets shiver clinging to the ground,
She's cold and blustering where once she wooed,
    And oftentimes in petulant tears is found;
But like sweet women, who sometimes are cross,
Her smiles come back the sweeter for their loss.

Good Cheer.

JUNE.

SHE sits all day plaiting a wild-rose wreath,
  This daughter of the Sun, come from afar.
  Sweeter is she than her bright sisters are
Who follow her across the flowery heath.
A daisy is her sign, and underneath
  The meadow's foamy flow the clovers wear
  Their uniforms of white and red, and bear
Their cups of sweet to scent their mistress' breath.
What dawns are thine, O dear, delicious June,
  When at the drawing of thy curtain's fold
The birds awake and sing a marvelous tune
  To the young Day that comes in rose and gold !
What twilights when the gray dusk hides thy face
That thou mayst come with more enchanting grace !
                              Travelers' Record.

GOLDEN-ROD.

LUCY LARCOM.

MIDSUMMER music in the grass—
  The cricket and the grasshopper;
White daisies and red clover pass;
  The caterpillar trails her fur
After the languid butterfly;
  But green and spring-like is the sod
Where autumn's earliest lamps I spy—
  The tapers of the golden-rod.

This flower is fuller of the sun
  Than any our pale North can show;
It has the heart of August won,
  And scatters wide the warmth and glow
Kindled at summer's mid-noon blaze,
  Where gentians of September bloom
Along October's leaf-strewn ways,
  And through November's paths of gloom.

As lavish of its golden light
  As sunshine's self, this blossom is;
Its starry chandeliers burn bright
  All day; and have you noted this—
A perfect sun in every flower,—
  Ten thousand thousand fairy suns,
Raying from new disks hour by hour,
  As up the stalk the life-flash runs?

Because its myriad glimmering plumes
  Like a great army's stir and wave,
Because its gold in billows blooms,
  The poor man's barren walks to lave;
Because its sun-shaped blossoms show
  How souls receive the light of God,
And unto earth give back that glow—
  I thank Him for the golden-rod.

———◆———

INDIAN SUMMER.

JOHN G. WHITTIER.

FROM gold to gray
  Our mild sweet day
Of Indian summer fades too soon;
  But tenderly
  Above the sea
Hangs, white and calm, the hunter's moon.

In its pale fire
  The village spire,
Shows like the zodiac's spectral lance,
  The painted walls
  Wheron it falls,
Transfigured stand in marble trance.

SEPTEMBER, 1815.

WILLIAM WORDSWORTH.

WHILE not a leaf seems faded, while the fields,
  With ripening harvests prodigally fair,
  In brightest sunshine bask, this nipping air,
Sent from some distant clime where Winter wields
His icy cimeter, a foretaste yields
  Of bitter change, and bids the flowers beware,
  And whispers to the silent birds, " Prepare
Against the threatening foe your trustiest shields."
For me, who, under kindlier laws, belong
  To Nature's tuneful choir, this rustling dry,
Through the green leaves, and yon crystalline sky,
  Announce a season potent to renew,
'Mid frost and snow, the instinctive joys of song,
And nobler cares than listless summer knew.

OCTOBER.

WILLIAM CULLEN BRYANT.

AY, thou art welcome, Heaven's delicious breath,
  When woods begin to wear the crimson leaf,
  And suns grow meek, and the meek suns grow brief,
And the year smiles as it draws near its death.
Wind of the sunny South, oh ! still delay
  In the gay woods and in the golden air,
  Like to a good old age released from care,
Journeying, in long serenity, away.
  In such a bright, late quiet, would that I
Might wear out life like thee, 'mid bowers and brooks,
And, dearer yet, the sunshine of kind looks,
  And music of kind voices ever nigh,
And, when my last sand twinkled in the glass,
Pass silently from men, as thou dost pass.

FADED LEAVES.

ALICE CARY.

THE hills are bright with maples yet;
  But down the level land
The beech-leaves rustle in the wind
  As dry and brown as sand.

The clouds in bars of rusty red
  Along the hilltops glow,
And in the still sharp air the frost
  Is like a dream of snow.

The berries of the brier rose
  Have lost their rounded pride,
The bitter-sweet chrysanthemums
  Are drooping heavy-eyed.

The cricket grows more friendly now,
  The dormouse sly and wise,
Hiding away in disgrace
  Of nature from men's eyes.

The pigeons in black and wavering lines
  Are swinging toward the sun;
And all the wide and withered fields
  Proclaim the summer done.

His store of nuts and acorns now
  The squirrel hastes to gain,
And sets his house in order for
  The winter's dreary reign.

'Tis time to light the evening fire,
  To read good books, to sing
The low and lovely songs that breathe
  Of the eternal spring.

NOVEMBER.

HARTLEY COLERIDGE.

THE mellow year is hasting to its close;
  The little birds have almost sung their last;
  Their small notes twitter in the dreary blast,
That shrill-piped harbinger of early snows;
The patient beauty of the scentless rose
  Oft with the morn's hoar crystal quaintly glassed
  Hangs a pale mourner for the summer past
And makes a little summer where it grows,
In the chill sunbeam of the faint, brief day.
  The dusky waters shudder as they shine;
  The russet leaves obstruct the straggling way
Of oozy brooks, which no deep banks confine,
And the gaunt woods, in ragged, scant array,
Wrap their old limbs with somber ivy-twine.

WINTER.

ROBERT SOUTHEY.

A WRINKLED, crabbed man they picture thee,
  Old Winter, with a rugged beard as gray
As the long moss upon the apple-tree;
Blue-lipt, an ice-drop at thy sharp blue nose,
  Close muffled up, and on thy dreary way
  Plodding alone through sleet and drifting snows.
They should have drawn thee by the high-heapt hearth,
Old Winter, seated in thy great armed chair,
  Watching the children at their Christmas mirth,
Or circled by them as thy lips declare
  Some merry jest, or tale of murder dire,
  Or troubled spirit that disturbs the night,
Pausing at times to rouse the moldering fire,
Or taste the old October brown and bright.

DECEMBER.

LOUISA PARSONS HOPKINS.

BLOW, northern winds !
To brace my fibers, knit my cords,
To gird my soul, to fire my words,
To do my work—for 'tis the Lord's—
To fashion minds.

Come, tonic blasts !
Arouse my courage, stir my thought,
Give nerve and strength that as I ought
I give my strength to what is wrought
While duty lasts.

Glow, arctic light !
And let my heart with burnished steel
That bright magnetic flame reveal
Which kindles purpose, faith, and zeal
For truth and right.

Shine, winter skies !
That when each brave day's work is done
I wait in peace from sun to sun,
To meet unshamed, through victory won,
Your starry eyes.

UNDER these names, January, February, March,
April, how much is hid that the eye cannot see ! Un-
cover the months and interpret them. In a low and
sweet way our Almanac began to speak as if he were a
harp, and as if the spirit of the year like a gentle wind
was breathing through it.—HENRY WARD BEECHER.

JANUARY.

ROSALINE E. JONES.

WHO can love you, January?
You are gruff and ugly—very.
          How you roar!
And a sorry tale you utter,
In a maniacal mutter,
          At my door.

Then you sob and sigh and pine,
In a mindless, minor whine,
          And again
A wild, grewsome ditty slips
From your frozen, rigid lips,
          Fierce as pain.

Like some creature strung to hate,
Wrestling with its cruel fate,
          Conquering
Only as you flee apace,
Glaring back with grim, wry face,
          Mimicking.

Hush your savage minstrelsy
To a mellower symphony,
          Soft and deep.
Know you no mellifluous rune?
No low, lulling cradle croon,
          Wooing sleep?

No soft breath from slumbrous isles,
Where eternal summer smiles
          Halcyon?
Beat your tattoo for your raids,
And decamp for Hadean shades.
          Pray begone!

FROST WORK.

MARY E. BRADLEY.

No fairies left? You need not tell me so,
　For in the night upon my window pane
Grew wondrous things that made me surely know
　The fairies are at their old tricks again.

O wonder working spirit! if I could
　But learn of you the secret of the snow—
How frost is given by the breath of God,
　And where the hidden water courses flow;

And where begotten is the dew that strings
　Her lovely pearls upon the meanest weed,
And what sweet animating influence brings
　The blossom splendid from the trivial seed;

Could I but ride the south wind and the north,
　And fathom all the mysteries they hold,
See how the lightning, leaping wildly forth,
　And how the turbulent thunder is controlled,

I would no more be fretted by the greed
　And selfishness of men; their puny spite,
Nor any worldly loss or cross indeed,
　My lifted soul could evermore affright.

And wherefore now? The laughing fairy seems
　To mock at me the spangled window through;
And I laugh also, waking from my dreams
　To take up daily loss and cross anew.

But with a sense of things divinely planned,
　That makes me sure I need not fear disdain,
From One who holds the thunder in his hand,
　Yet stoops to trace the frost work on the pane.

FLOWERS.

No Flowers.

How bleak and drear the earth would seem
   Were there no flower faces
To give the hills, the woods and fields
   Their pleasing charms and graces!
Could spring be spring without a flower
   To smile at April's weeping?
Would robins trill so gay a song,
   Or May day be worth keeping?

And only think how bare the hedge
   Would look without its posies!—
How queer 'twould be to have a June
   That did not smell like roses!
No dandelions on the sward
   For childhood's busy fingers;
No morning-glories, drinking dew,
   While golden sunrise lingers!

No violets, with hoods of blue,
   To nod at mild spring's coming;
No clover blossoms—would we hear
   The busy bees' soft humming?
And were there no forget-me-nots,
   No buttercups or daisies,
The children would be lost for sports,
   The poet lost for phrases.

No flowers, with their refining power
   No wafts from yon sweet heaven—
No tokens of a love divine
   To erring mortals given!

Ah, flowers your smiling faces prove
The Source of all our pleasures
Would not pronounce creation good
Without thee, floral treasures !

FERNS.

FERNS, beautiful ferns,
 By the side of the running waters,
Lovely and sweet and fresh,
 As the fairest of earth-born daughters;
Under the dreamy shade
 Of the forest's mighty branches,
Curving their graceful shapes
 To the playful wind's advances.

Ferns, delicate ferns,
 Neighbors of emerald mosses,
Having no thought or care
 For worldly attainments or losses.
Children of shadow serene,
 Fresh at the heart through the summer,
Over the cool springs they lean,
 Where the sunbeam is rarely a comer.

Ferns, feathery ferns,
 Delicate, slender and frail,
Nursed by the streamlet, whose song
 Is music for hillside and vale.
Purity, modesty, grace,
 Emblems of these to the mind,
Loving the quietest place
 That ever a sunbeam will find.

SWEET PEAS.

OH, what is the use of such pretty wings
   If one never, never can fly?
Pink and fine as the clouds that shine
   In the delicate morning sky.
With a perfume sweet as the lilies keep
Down in their vases so white and deep.

The brown bees go humming aloft;
   The humming-bird soars away;
The butterfly blows like the leaf of a rose,
   Off, off in the sunshine gay;
While you peep over the garden wall,
Looking so wistfully after them all.

Are you tired of the company
   Of the balsams so dull and proud?
Of the coxcombs bold and the marigold,
   And the spider-wort wrapped in a cloud?
Have you not plenty of sunshine and dew,
And crowds of gay gossips to visit you?

How you flutter, and reach, and climb!
   How eager your wee faces are!
Aye, turned to the light till the blind old night
   Is led to the world by a star.
Well, it surely is hard to feel one's wings,
And still be prisoned like wingless things.

"Tweet, tweet," then says Parson Thrush,
   Who is preaching up in a tree;
"Though you never may fly while the world goes by,
   Take heart, little flowers," says he;
" For often, I know, to the souls that aspire
   Comes something better than their desire!"

St. Nicholas.

THE TRAILING ARBUTUS.

JOHN G. WHITTIER.

I WANDERED lone where the pine trees made
Against the east their barricade;
 And, guided by its sweet
Perfume, I found within a narrow dell
The trailing spring flower, tinted like a shell,
 Amid dry leaves and mosses at my feet.

From under dead boughs, for whose loss the pines
Moaned ceasless overhead, the blossoming vines
 Lifted their glad surprise,
While yet the bluebird smoothed in leafless trees
His feathers, ruffled by chill sea breeze,
 And snowdrifts lingered under April skies.

As, pausing, o'er the lowly flowers I bent,
I thought of lives thus lowly, clogged and pent,
 Which yet find room,
Through care and cumber, coldness and decay,
To lend a sweetness to the ungenial day,
 And make the sad earth happier for their bloom.

A BUNCH OF COWSLIPS.

IN the rarest of English valleys
 A motherless girl ran wild,
And the greenness and silence and gladness
 Were soul of the soul of the child.
The birds were her gay little brothers,
 The squirrels her sweethearts shy;
And her heart kept tune with the raindrops,
 And sailed with the clouds in the sky;
And angels kept coming and going,
 With beautiful things to do;
And wherever they left a footprint,
 A cowslip or primrose grew.

She was taken to live in London—
  So thick with pitiless folk—
And she could not smile for its badness,
  And could not breathe for its smoke;
And now as she lay on her pallet,
  Too weary and weak to rise,
A smile of ineffable longing
  Brought dews to her faded eyes;
"Oh, me! for a yellow cowslip,
  A pale little primrose dear!
Won't some kind angel remember,
  And pluck one and bring it here?"

They brought her a bunch of cowslips;
  She took them with fingers weak,
And kissed them, and stroked them, and loved them,
  And laid them against her cheek.
"It was kind of the angels to send them;
  And now I'm too tired to pray,
If God looks down at the cowslips,
  He'll know what I want to say."
They buried them in her bosom;
  And when she shall wake and rise,
Why may not the flowers be quickened,
  And bloom in her happy skies?

———◆———

DAFFODILS.

ROBERT HERRICK.

WE have short time to stay as you,
  We have as short a spring;
As quick a growth, to meet decay,
  As you or anything.
    We die
As your hours do, and dry
    Away,
  Like to the summer's rain,
Or as the pearls of morning's dew,
  Ne'er to be found again.

CHRYSANTHEMUMS.

MRS. MARY E. DODGE.

BRAVEST of brave sweet blossoms in all of the garden-row;
Fair, when most of the flowers shrink from the winds that
blow;
Gay, when the dismal north wind wails through the tree-tops
dumb;
Breathing a breath of gladness is the brave Chrysanthemum.

One is of tawny color; another of cardinal glow,
As the cheek of a sun-warmed maiden and reddest of wine
will show;
While some are of gorgeous yellow, like gold in a monarch's
crown,
And some of a royal purple, dusted with softest down.

Some of a creamy whiteness, touched to a rosy blush,
As the snow of the lovely Jungfrau glows with a sunset flush;
Some flame at the heart, pearl-petaled; and lavender-hued
are some;
Yet each of them, crude or cultured, just a brave Chrysanthe-
mum.

ROSES.

IT is summer, says a fairy,
Bring me tissue light and airy;
Bring me colors of the rarest,
Search the rainbow for the fairest
Sea-shell, pink and sunny yellow,
Kingly crimson, deep and mellow;
Faint red in Aurora beaming,
And the white in pure pearl gleaming.

Bring me diamonds from the spaces
Where the air the earth embraces;
Bring me gold-dust by divining
Where the humming-bird is mining;

Bring me sweets as rich as may be
From the kisses of a baby;
With an art no fay discloses
I am going to make some roses.

THE MESSAGE OF THE SNOWDROP.

COURAGE and hope, true heart !
   Summer is coming though late the spring,
Over the breast of the quiet mold,
   With an emerald shimmer—a glint of gold,
Till the leaves of the regal rose unfold
   At the rush of the swallow's wing.

Courage and hope, true heart !
   Summer is coming though spring be late;
Wishing is weary and waiting is long,
But sorrow's day hath an even-song,
And the garlands that never shall fade belong
   To the soul that is strong to wait.

RAGGED SAILORS.

O RAGGED, ragged Sailors !
   I pray you answer me:
What may you all be doing
   So far away from sea ?

" We're loitering by the roadsides,
   We're lingering on the hills,
To talk with pretty Daisies
   In stiff and snowy frills.

" And though our blue be ragged,
   Right welcome still are we
To tell the nodding lasses
   Long tales about the sea !"

DIALOGUES.

THE QUEEN'S NECKLACE.

ALEXANDER DUMAS.

NOTE.—The scandal concerning this famous necklace—upon which the story is founded—was one of the many misfortunes endured by the unhappy Queen Marie Antoinette.

Characters: { MARIE ANTOINETTE. Queen of France.
{ Monsieur BOEHMER, Merchant.

Monsieur Boehmer. We do not come to offer anything to your Majesty, we should fear to be indiscreet; but we come to fulfill a duty concerning the necklace which your Majesty did not deign to take.

Marie Antoinette. Oh! then the necklace has come again! It was really beautiful, M. Boehmer.

M. B. So beautiful that your Majesty alone was worthy to wear it.

M. A. My consolation is that it cost a million and a half francs, and in these times there is no sovereign that can give such a sum for a necklace; so that although I cannot wear it, no one else can.

M. B. That is an error of your Majesty's. The necklace is sold.

M. A. Sold! To whom?

M. B. Ah, Madame, that is a state secret.

M. A. Oh, I think I am safe. A state secret means that there is nothing to tell.

M. B. With your Majesty we do not act as with others. The necklace is sold, but in the most secret manner, and an embassador—

15

M. A. I really think you believe it yourself! Come, M. Boehmer, tell me at least the country he comes from, or, at all events, the first letter of his name.

M. B. Madame, it is the embassador from Portugal.

M. A. The embassador from Portugal! There is none here, M. Boehmer.

M. B. He came expressly for this, Madame.

M. A. Well, so much the better for the Queen of Portugal. We will speak of it no more.

M. B. We could not let the diamonds leave France without expressing our regret to your Majesty. It is a necklace which is now known all over Europe, and we wished to know definitely that your Majesty really refused it before we parted with it.

M. A. My refusal has been made public, and has been too much applauded for me to repent it.

M. B. Oh, Madame, if the people found it admirable that your Majesty preferred a ship of war to a necklace, the nobility at least would not think it surprising if you bought the necklace after all.

M. A. Do not speak of it any more!

M. B. It has touched your Majesty's neck; it ought not to belong to any one else. We will return to-morrow.

M. A. Impossible! I have amused myself with these jewels; to do more would be a fault.

M. B. Your Majesty, then, refuses them?

M. A. Yes, oh yes. Take the necklace back. Put it away immediately!

QUEEN ISABELLA'S RESOLVE.

EPES SARGENT.

Characters:
{ ISABELLA, QUEEN OF SPAIN.
{ DON GOMEZ, a Grandee.
{ CHRISTOPHER COLUMBUS.

Isabella. And so, Don Gomez, you think we ought to dismiss the proposition of this worthy Genoese?

Don Gomez. His scheme, your Majesty, is fanciful in the extreme. I am a plain man. I do not see visions and dream dreams like some men.

I. And yet Columbus has given us good reasons for believing that he can reach India by sailing in a westerly direction.

D. G. Delusion, your Majesty! Admitting that the earth is a sphere, how would it be possible for him to return, if he once descended the sphere in the direction he proposes? Would not the coming back be all up-hill? Could a ship accomplish it even with the most favorable wind?

I. What have you to say to these objections, Columbus?

Col. With your Majesty's leave, I would suggest that if the earth is a sphere, the same laws of adhesion and motion must operate at every point on its surface.

D. G. Don't try to make *me*, a grandee of Spain, believe such stuff as that there are people on the earth who walk with their heads down, like flies on a ceiling! Would not the blood run into my head if I were standing upside down?

Col. I have already answered that objection. If there are people on the earth who are our antipodes, it should be remembered that we are also theirs.

I. To cut short the discussion, you think that the enterprise, which Columbus proposes, is one unworthy of our serious consideration?

D. G. As a matter-of-fact man, I must confess that I do so regard it. Has your Majesty ever seen an embassador from this unknown coast?

I. Have you ever seen an embassador from the unknown world of spirits?

D. G. Certainly not. Through faith we look forward to it.

I. Even so, by faith, does Columbus look forward, far over the misty ocean, to an undiscovered shore. Know, Don Gomez, that the *absurdity*, as you style it, shall be tested, and that forthwith.

D. G. Your Majesty will excuse me if I remark that I have from your royal consort himself the assurance that the finances of the government are so exhausted by the late wars that he cannot consent to advance the necessary funds for fitting out an expedition of the kind proposed.

I. Be mine, then, the privilege! I have jewels, by the pledging of which I can raise the amount required; and I have resolved that they shall be pledged to this enterprise without more delay.

Col. Your Majesty shall not repent your heroic resolve. I will return—be sure I will return—and lay at your feet such a jewel as never queen wore yet, an imperishable fame that shall couple with your memory the benedictions of millions yet unborn in climes yet unknown to civilized man. There is a conviction in my mind that your Majesty will live to bless the hour you came to this decision.

THE MILL ON THE FLOSS.

GEORGE ELIOT.

Characters: { TOM TULLIVER.
{ MAGGIE TULLIVER.

Maggie. I'll help you now, Tom. I've come to the school to stay ever so long. I've brought my box and my pinafores—haven't I, father?

Tom. You help me, you silly little thing! I should like to see you doing one of my lessons. Why, I learn Latin, too. Girls never learn such things. They're too silly.

M. I know what Latin is very well. Latin's a language. There are Latin words in the dictionary. There's *bonus*, a gift.

T. Now you're just wrong there, Miss Maggie. You think you're very wise. But "bonus" means "good," as it happens—bonus, bona, bonum.

M. Well, that's no reason why it shouldn't mean "gift." It may mean several things—almost every word does. There's "lawn"—it means the grass-plot as well as the stuff pocket-handkerchiefs are made of.

T. Now, then, come with me into the study, Maggie.

M. Oh, what books! How I should like to have as many books as that!

T. Why, you couldn't read one of 'em. They're all Latin.

M. No, they aren't. I can read the back of this, "History of the Decline and Fall of the Roman Empire."

T. Well, what does that mean? *You* don't know.

M. But I could soon find out. I should look inside and see what it was about.

T. Oh, I say, Maggie, we must keep quiet here, you know. If we break anything, we'll have to cry **peccavi.**

M. What's that?

T. It's the Latin for a good scolding.

M. Is your Mrs. Stelling a cross woman, Tom?

T. I believe you!

M. I think all women are crosser than men. Aunt Glegg's a great deal crosser than Uncle Glegg, and mother scolds me more than father does.

T. Well, you'll be a woman some day, so *you* needn't talk.

M. But *I* shall be a *clever* woman, Tom.

T. Oh, I dare say, and a nasty conceited thing. Everybody'll hate you.

M. But you oughtn't to hate me, Tom. It will be very wicked of you, for I shall be your sister.

T. Oh, bother! Come, it's time for me to learn my lessons. Just see what I've got to do!

Characters: { Mrs. TULLIVER.
               Mrs. PULLET.

Mrs. P. My new bonnet has come home, Bessy.

Mrs. T. Has it, sister? And how do you like it?

Mrs. P. It's apt to make a mess with clothes, taking them out and puting them in again. But it would be a pity for you to go away without seeing it. There's no knowing what may happen.

Mrs. T. I'm afraid it'll be troublesome to you getting it out, sister; but I should like to see what kind of a crown she's made you.

Mrs. P. You'd like to see it on, sister? I'll open the shutter a bit farther.

Mrs. T. Well, if you don't mind taking off your cap, sister.

Mrs. P. I've sometimes thought there's a loop too much of ribbon on the left side, sister. What do *you* think?

Mrs. T. Well, I think it's best as it is. If you meddled with it, sister, you might repent. How much might she charge you for that bonnet, sister?

Mrs. P. Pullet pays for it. He said I was to have the best bonnet at Garum Church, let the next best be whose it would. I may never wear it twice, sister; who knows?

Mrs. T. Don't talk of that, sister. I hope you'll keep your health this summer.

Mrs. P. But there may come a death in the family, as there did soon after I had my green satin bonnet.

Mrs. T. That *would* be unlucky. There's never so much pleasure in wearing a bonnet a second year, especially when the crowns are so chancy—never two summers alike.

Mrs. P. Ah, it's the way of the world! Sister, if you should never see that bonnet again till I'm dead and gone, you'll remember I showed it to you this very day.

THE HILLS OF THE SHATEMUC.

SUSAN WARNER.

Characters: { RUFUS LANDHOLM.
{ WINTHROP LANDHOLM.

Rufus. We've got the farm in pretty good order now.

Winthrop. Yes, father has, if those stumps were once out. We ought to have good crops this year of most things.

R. I am sure I have spent four or five years of *my* life in hard work upon it.

W. Your life ain't much the worse for it. Father has spent more than that. How hard he has worked—to make this farm !

R. It was a pretty tough subject to begin with; but now it's the handsomest farm in the county. It ought to pay considerable after this.

W. It hasn't brought us in much so far, Rufus, except just to keep along; and a pretty tight fit at that.

R. If the farm was clear, I'd stand the chance of its paying. It's that keeps us down—the debt.

W. Debt ! What debt?

R. The interest on the mortgage.

W. What is the debt ?

R. Several thousands, I believe.

W. You and I must pay off that money, Rufus.

R. Ay; but still there's the question, which is the best way to do it ?

W. The best way, I've a notion, is not to take too long noon-spells in the afternoon.

R. Stop a bit. Sit down again; I want to speak to you. Do you want to spend all your life following the oxen ?

W. What is the matter, Rufus ?

R. Matter ! Why, Winthrop, that I am not willing to stay here and be a ploughman all my life, when I might be something better.

W. How can you be anything better, Rufus ?

R. Do you think all the world is like this little world which these hills shut in ? There is another sort of world, Winthrop, where people know something; where other things are to be done than running plough furrows; where men may read and write—do something great—distinguish themselves. I want to be in that world.

W. But what will you do, Rufus, to get into that world? We are shut in here.

R. *I* am not shut in! I will live for something greater than this!

W. So would I, if I could; but what are we to do?

R. There is only one thing to do. I shall go to college.

W. But some preparation is necessary, Rufus; isn't it? How will you get that? Father wants us this summer. We are just beginning to help him.

R. We can help him much better the other way. Farming is the most miserable slow way of making money that ever was contrived.

W. How do *you* propose to make money, Rufus?

R. I don't know. I am not thinking about making money at present.

W. It takes a great deal to go to college, don't it?

R. Yes. But I intend to go, Winthrop.

W. Yes, you'll go.

R. I'll *try* for it.

W. *And you'll get it, too,* Rufus!

MISTRESS AND MAID.

DINAH MULOCK CRAIK.

Characters: { SELINA LEAF. HILARY LEAF.

Selina. I'm sure I don't know how we are to manage with Elizabeth. That greedy—

Hilary. And growing—

S. I say that greedy girl eats as much as both of us. And as for her clothes—her mother doesn't keep her decent.

H. She would find it hard on three pounds a year.

S. Hilary, how dare you contradict me? I am only stating a plain fact.

H. And I another. But, indeed, I don't want to talk, Selina.

S. You never do except when you are wished to be silent, and then your tongue goes like any race-horse.

H. Does it? Well, like Gilpin's,

> "It carries weight, it rides a race,
> 'Tis for a thousand pound!"

—and I only wish it were. Heigh-ho! If I could but earn a thousand pounds!

S. I'm sure she was as black as a chimney-sweep all to-day. Her pinafore had three rents in it, which she never thinks of mending, though I gave her needles and thread myself a week ago. She doesn't know how to use them any more than a baby.

H. Possibly nobody ever taught her.

S. Yes, she went for a year to the National School, she says.

H. Well, her forte is certainly children. She is wonderfully patient with our troublesome scholars.

S. You always find something to say for her.

H. I should be ashamed if I could not find something to say for anybody who is always abused. How can I help it, Selina, if a girl fifteen years old is not a paragon of perfection? as we all are, if we only could find it out.

S. Her month ends to-morrow. Let her go.

H. And perhaps get in her place a story-teller, a tale-bearer, even a thief. By the bye, the first step in the civilization of the Polynesians was giving them clothes. Suppose we try the experiment with Elizabeth?

THE LAST DAYS OF POMPEII.

EDWARD BULWER LYTTON.

City destroyed, A.D. August 24, 79. Discovered, 1750.

Characters: { CLODIUS, PAUSA, } Citizens.

Clodius. When is our next wild-beast fight?

Pausa. It stands fixed for the ninth ide of August. We have a most lovely young lion for the occasion.

C. Whom shall we get for him to eat? Alas! there is a great scarcity of criminals. You must positively find some innocent or other to condemn to the lion, Pausa.

P. Indeed, I have thought very seriously about it of late. It was a most infamous law which forbade us to send our own slaves to the wild beasts. Not to let us do what we like with our own! That's what I call an infringement on property itself.

C. Not so in the good old days of the Republic.

P. And then this pretended mercy to the slaves is such a disappointment to the poor people. How they do love to see a good tough battle between a man and a lion! And all this innocent pleasure they may lose—if the gods don't send us a good criminal soon—from this cursed law.

C. What can be worse policy than to interfere with the manly amusements of the people?

P. Well, thank Jupiter and the Fates! We have no Nero at present.

C. He was, indeed, a tyrant. He shut up our amphi-theatre for ten years.

P. I wonder it didn't create a rebellion.

C. As it very nearly did.

Characters: { GLAUCUS, SALLUST, LEPIDUS, } Citizens.

Sallust. Ah, it is a lustrum since I saw you!

Glaucus. And how have you spent the lustrum? What new dishes have you discovered?

S. I have been scientific, and have made some experiments in the feeding of lampreys. I confess I despair of bringing them to the perfection which our Roman ancestors attained.

G. Miserable man! and why?

S. Because it is no longer lawful to give them a slave to eat. But slaves are not slaves nowadays, and have no sympathy with their masters' interest, or one of mine would destroy himself to oblige me.

Lepidus. What news from Rome?

S. The emperor has been giving a splendid supper to the senators.

L. He is a good creature. They say he never sends a man away without granting his request.

S. Perhaps he would let me kill a slave for my reservoir?

G. Not unlikely; for he who grants a favor to one Roman must always do it at the expense of another. Be sure that for every smile Titus has caused a hundred eyes have wept.

S. Long live Titus! He has promised my brother a quæstorship because he has run through his fortune.

L. And wishes now to enrich himself among the people.

S. Exactly so.

G. That is putting the people to some use. Well, let us to the baths. This is the time when all the world is there, and Fulvius, whom you admire so much, is going to read us an ode.

RUTH HALL.

F A N N Y F E R N.

Characters: { Mrs. HENRY HALL.
{ Mrs. RUTH HALL, Daughter-in-law.

Mrs. H. Good morning, Ruth; *Mrs. Hall,* I suppose, I *should* call you, only that I can't get used to being shoved aside so suddenly.

Ruth. Oh, pray don't say Mrs. Hall to *me.* Call me any name that best pleases you; I shall be quite satisfied.

Mrs. H. I suppose you understand all about housekeeping, Ruth?

Ruth. No. I have but just returned from boarding-school.

Mrs. H. It is a great pity you were not brought up properly. Harry has his fortune yet to make, you know. Young people nowadays seem to think money comes in showers. Harry has been brought up sensibly. He has been taught economy. Do you know how to iron, Ruth?

Ruth. Yes. I have sometimes clear-starched my own muslins and laces.

Mrs. H. Glad to hear it. Can you make bread? When I say *bread,* I *mean* bread,—none of your soda, saleratus mixtures,—old-fashioned yeast-*riz* bread. Do you know how to make it?

Ruth. No. People in the city always buy baker's bread; my father did.

Mrs. H. Your father! Land's sake, child, you mustn't quote your father, now you're married. I hope you won't be always running home, or running anywhere, in fact. Do you know I should like your looks better if you didn't curl your hair?

Ruth. I don't curl it; it curls naturally.

Mrs. H. That's a pity. You should avoid everything that looks frivolous. And, Ruth, if you should feel the need of exercise, don't gad in the streets. There is nothing like a broom and a dust-pan to make the blood circulate. I hope you don't read novels and such trash. I have a very select little library containing a most excellent sermon on Predestination by our good old minister, Dr. Diggs. Any time you stand in need of *rational* reading, come to me.

-----◆-----

DIOGENES AND PLATO ON PRIDE.

T. A. BLAND.

Diogenes. Fie on thy philosophy, Plato! In spite of all, thou art the veriest of aristocrats, while philosophy teacheth humility.

Plato. Thou hast spoken truly, Diogenes, but not in wisdom; thy speech is wise, 'tis true, but thy thought is foolish. That I am proud, I own, and that I am a democrat, I do most sincerely maintain.

D. Now thou speakest in riddles. Thy words are double, and thy answer as the answer of the fool.

P. Gently, Diogenes. Anger not thy mind with quick speech that is void of wisdom. Let us inquire into this matter with the calmness and deliberation befitting the dignity of philosophy. Is not pride self-respect, and is not self-respect an admirable virtue?

D. Nay, nay, Plato. Thou art surely in the wrong here. Pride is vanity, and it leadeth to contempt for the merits of thy fellows. Thus is aristocracy fostered.

P. If it were as you affirm, then would I quickly

eschew pride. But I do not so hold, nor did Socrates. Methinks it were vanity, and not pride, thou wouldst condemn, Diogenes, and pride and vanity, I hold, are very different matters.

D. Thy reasons? Give me thy reasons for this opinion. I do maintain that pride is the root and substance of vanity.

P. Then thou dost surely not think wisely. To be proud is to esteem one's self, while the vain man is anxious about the praise of the mob. Pride is self-reliant, confident, courageous. Vanity is fawning, anxious, and cowardly. And thou, too, art proud, Diogenes. Thy contempt for what thou callest my pride is the offspring of thy greater pride. Thou believest in the wisdom of Diogenes more than in that of Plato. Is not this thy pride?

D. But Plato lives in a palace and clothes his person with costly raiment. Diogenes despiseth costly raiment and lives in a tub.

P. Diogenes is therefore shown to be not only prouder than Plato, but vainer also.

D. Vain, dost thou say, Plato? Art in thy right mind to call Diogenes vain?

P. I call thee vain, Diogenes, and if thou but hear me I will prove it. Thou art vain of thy fame, for thou art famous for thy humility. Thou art proud of thy wisdom, also, Diogenes, and vain of thy learning. Thou thinkest that thou art wiser than Plato, else thou wouldst become his disciple; and richer than Alexander, else thou wouldst not scorn his gifts. 'Tis Diogenes who is the aristocrat. He thinks himself better than others, and is therefore above his fellows.

D. Hold thee there, Plato. Thou surely doest me wrong. Do I not live like a peasant, and scorn only

the rich and they that are in high places; and is that
pride?

P. Thou dost indeed wear the garb of a peasant, but
thou also carriest a lantern to search for an honest man,
boldly proclaiming that until such a man is found thou
wilt live alone. Is not this virtuous aristocracy? Fie
on thy democracy, Diogenes! By thine own argument
thou art a greater aristocrat than Plato. But learn this,
and add it to thy stock of wisdom: True pride is con-
sistent with philosophy, and philosophy is the foe of
vanity.

LORNA DOONE.

R. D. BLACKMORE.

Place, London; time, about 1680; reign of James II.

Characters: { JOHN RIDD, a countryman.
{ Judge GEORGE JEFFREYS, Lord Chief Justice of England.

J. R. May it please your worship, here I am, according to order, awaiting your good pleasure.

J. J. Thou art made to weight, John, more than order. How much dost thou tip the scales to?

J. R. Only twelve score pounds, my lord, when I be
in wrestling trim. And sure I must have lost weight
here, fretting so long in London.

J. J. Ha, much fret there is in thee! Has his Majesty seen thee?

J. R. Yes, my lord, twice, or even thrice, and he
made some jest concerning me.

J. J. A very poor one, I doubt not. Now, is there
in thy neighborhood at Exmoor a certain nest of robbers,
miscreants, and outlaws, whom all men fear to handle?

J. R. Yes, my lord; at least I believe some of them
be robbers; and all of them are outlaws.

J. J. And what is your high-sheriff about that he doth not hang them all? Or send them up for me to hang, without more to do about it?

J. R. I reckon that he is afraid, my lord. It is not safe to meddle with them. They are of good birth, and reckless, and their place is very strong.

J. J. Good birth! What was Lord Russell of, Lord Essex, and Sidney? 'Tis the surest heirship to the block to be the chip of an old one. What is the name of this pestilent race, and how many of them are there?

J. R. They are the Doones of Bagworthy Forest, may it please your worship. And we reckon there be about forty of them, besides the women and children.

J. J. Forty Doones all forty thieves! How long have they been there, then?

J. R. Before the great war they came, longer back than I can remember.

J. J. Ay, long before thou wast born, John. Good, thou speakest plainly. Woe betide a liar, whenso I get hold of him. Ye need me on the Western Circuit, and ye shall have me when London traitors are hung and swung. Now, a few more things, John Ridd, and, for the present, I have done with thee. Is there any sound, round your way of disaffection to his most gracious Majesty?

J. R. No, my lord; no sign whatever. We pray for him in church, and talk about him afterward, hoping it may do him good, as it is intended. But after that we have naught to say, not knowing much about him—at least till I get home again.

J. J. That is as it should be, John, and the less you say the better. Now, John, I have taken a liking to thee; for never man told me the truth, without fear or favor, more truly than thou hast done. I meant to

16

use thee as my tool, but thou art too honest and simple; and never let me find thee, John, a tool for the other side, or a tube for my words to pass through.

———◆———

THE MUSICAL INSTRUMENT.

Characters: { AUNT TABITHA.
LAURA.

A. T. Thy grandmother, child, thy grandmother used to play upon a much better instrument than thine.

L. Indeed; how could it have been better? You know a piano is the most fashionable instrument, and is used by everybody that is *anything*.

A. T. Thy grandmother was *something*, yet she never saw a piano-forte.

L. But what was the name of the instrument? Had it strings, and was it played by the hand?

A. T. You must give me time to recollect the name. It was, indeed, a stringed instrument, and was played with the hand.

L. By the hands alone? How vulgar! But I should really like to see one, and papa must buy me one when I return to the city. Do you think we can obtain one?

A. T. No; you probably will not obtain one there; but, doubtless, they may be found in some of the country towns.

L. How many strings had it? Must one play with both hands? And could one play the double-bass?

A. T. I know not whether it would play the double-bass, as you call it; but it was played with both hands, and had two strings.

L. Two strings only? Surely you are jesting! How could good music be procured from such an instrument, when the piano has two or three hundred?

A. T. Oh, the strings were very long, one of them about fourteen feet, and the other may be lengthened at pleasure, even to fifty feet or more.

L. What a prodigious deal of room it must take up! But no matter. I will have mine in the old hall, and papa may have an addition built to it, for he says I shall never want for anything, and so does mamma. But what kind of sound did it make? Were the strings struck with little mallets, like the piano? or were they snapped like a harp?

A. T. Like neither of those instruments, as I recollect; but it produced a soft kind of humming music, and was peculiarly agreeable to the husband and relations of the performer.

L. Oh, as to pleasing one's husband or relations, you know that is altogether vulgar in fashionable society. But I am determined to have one, at any rate. Was it easily learned? and was it taught by French and Italian masters?

A. T. It was easily learned, but taught neither by Frenchmen nor Italians.

L. Can you not possibly remember the name? How shall we know what to inquire for?

A. T. Yes. I do now remember the name, and you must inquire for a Spinning-wheel.

PUT YOURSELF IN HIS PLACE.

A STORY OF THE TRADES-UNIONS.

CHARLES READE.

Characters: { Mr. GROTAIT, Proprietor of The Cutlers' Arms.
{ HENRY LITTLE, Inventor, and Manufacturer of Cutlers' Tools.

Mr. G. Well, Mr. Little, now, between ourselves, don't you think it rather hard that the poor workman should have to hang and race the master's grindstone for nothing?

Mr. L. Why, they share the loss between them. The stone costs the master three pounds, and hanging it only costs the workman four or five shillings. Where's the grievance?

Mr. G. Hanging and racing a stone shortens the grinder's life; fills his lungs with grit. Is the workman to give Life and Labor for a forenoon, and is Capital to contribute nothing? Is that your view of Life, Labor, and Capital, young man?

Mr. L. That is smart; but a rule of trade is a rule till it is altered by consent of the parties that made it. Now, right or wrong, it is the rule of trade here that the small grinders find their own stones and pay for power. Cheetham is smarting under your rules, and you can't expect him to go against any rule that saves him a shilling.

Mr. G. What does this grinder—Cheetham—think?

Mr. L. You might as well ask what the grindstone thinks.

Mr. G. Well, what does the grinder *say*, then?

Mr. L. Says he'd rather run the old stone out than lose a forenoon.

Mr. G. Well, sir, it is his business.

Mr. L. It may be a man's business to hang himself; but it is the bystanders' to hinder him.

Mr. G. You mistake me. I mean that the grinder is the only man who knows whether a stone is safe.

Mr. L. But this grinder does not pretend his stone is safe; all he says is, safe or not, he'll run it. So now the question is, will you pay four shillings yourself for this blockhead's loss of time in hanging and racing a new stone? Your Union can find money. Why grudge it when there's life to be saved, perhaps, and ten times cheaper than you pay for blood?

Mr. G. Young man, did you come here to insult us with these worn-out slanders?

Mr. L. No; but I came to see whether you secretaries, who can find pounds to assassinate men and blow up women and children with gunpowder, can find shillings to secure the life of one of your own members.

Mr. G. Well, sir, the application is without precedent, and I must decline it; but this I beg to do as courteously as the application has been made uncourteously.

Mr. L. Oh, it is easy to be polite when you've got no heart.

Mr. G. You are the first ever brought that charge against me. Now, have you nothing to say to us on your own account?

Mr. L. Not a word!

Mr. G. But suppose I could suggest a way by which you could carry on your trade here and offend nobody?

Mr. L. I should decline to hear it. You and I are at war on that. You have done your worst, and I shall do my best to make you all smart for it, the moment I get a chance.

Mr. G. So be it, then!

———◆———

PILGRIM'S PROGRESS.

JOHN BUNYAN.

Characters: $\left\{ \begin{array}{l} \text{FAITHFUL,} \\ \text{TALKATIVE,} \end{array} \right\}$ Pilgrims.

Faith. Friend, whither away? Are you going to the Heavenly Country?

Talk. I am going to the same place.

F. That is well. Then I hope we may have your good company.

T. With a very good will will I be your companion.

F. Come on then, and let us go together, and let us spend our time in discoursing of things that are profitable.

T. To talk of things that are good, to me is very acceptable, with you or with any other; for to speak the truth, there are but few who care thus to spend their time, but choose much rather to be speaking of things to no profit, and this hath been a trouble to me.

F. That is indeed a thing to be lamented; for what things so worthy of the use of the tongue and mouth of men on earth as are the things of the God of Heaven?

T. I like you wonderful well, for your saying is full of conviction. What things so pleasant?—that is, if a man hath any delight in things that are wonderful. If, for instance, a man doth delight to talk of the History or the Mystery of things.

F. That's true; but to be profited by such things in our talk, should be that which we design.

T. That's it that I said. Further, by this a man may learn to refute false opinions, to vindicate the truth, and also to instruct the ignorant.

F. All this is true, and glad am I to hear these things from you. Well then, what is that one thing that we shall at this time found our discourse upon?

T. What you will. I will talk of things Heavenly, or things Earthly; things Moral, or things Evangelical; things Sacred, or things Profane; things past, or things to come; things foreign, or things at home; things more Essential, or things Circumstantial; provided that all be done to our profit.

F. Doth your life and conversation testify to Faith,

Love, and Grace? or standeth your Religion in Word or
in Tongue, and not in Deed and Truth? Pray if you
incline to answer me in this, say no more than you know
the God above will say *Amen* to; and also nothing but
what your conscience can justify you in.

T. This kind of talk I did not expect; nor am I in-
clined to give an answer to such questions, because I
count not myself bound thereto, unless you take upon
you to be a Catechizer; and though you should do so,
yet I may refuse to make you my Judge. But, I pray, will
you tell me why you ask me such questions?

F. Because I saw you forward to talk, and because I
knew that you had naught else but notion.

T. Since you judge so rashly as you do, I cannot but
conclude you are some peevish or melancholy man, not
fit to be discoursed with; and so adieu.

ALTON LOCKE, TAILOR AND POET.

CHARLES KINGSLEY.

Characters: { Mr. CROSSTHWAITE. Tailor.
ALTON LOCKE, Tailor's Apprentice.
Time, 1830.

A. L. Mr. Crossthwaite, I want to speak to you. I
want you to advise me.

Mr. C. I have known that a long time.

A. L. Then why did you never say a kind word to
me?

Mr. C. I was waiting to see whether you were worth
it. Besides, I wanted to see whether you trusted me
enough to ask me. Now you've broke the ice at last,
in with you head and ears, and see what you can fish
out.

A. L. I am very unhappy.

Mr. C. That's no new disorder, as I know of.

A. L. No; but I think the reason I am unhappy is a strange one; at least, I never read of but one person else in the same way. I want to educate myself and I can't.

Mr. C. You must have read precious little, then, if you think yourself in a strange way. Bless the boy's heart! And what the dickens do you want to be educating yourself for? If you had one-tenth the trouble taken with you that is taken with every pig-headed son of an aristocrat—

A. L. Am I clever?

Mr. C. Clever? What, haven't you found that out yet? Don't try to put that on me!

A. L. Really, I never thought of it.

Mr. C. More simpleton you! I heard said the other day that you were a thorough young genius.

A. L. It sounds very grand, and I should certainly like to have a good education. But I can't see whose injustice keeps me out of one if I can't afford to pay for it.

Mr. C. Whose? Why, the parsons', to be sure. They've got the monopoly of education in England, and get their bread by it. Of course, it's their interest to keep up the price of their commodity, and let no man have a taste of it who can't pay down handsomely.

A. L. But I thought the clergy were doing so much to help the poor. At least, I hear all the dissenting ministers grumbling at their continual interference.

Mr. C. Ay, educating them to make them slaves and bigots. They don't teach them what they teach their own sons.

A. L. But there are countless stories of great Englishmen who have risen from the lowest ranks.

Mr. C. Ay; but where are the stories of those who have not risen? Dead men tell no tales; and this old whited sepulcher, society, ain't going to turn informer against itself.

A. L. I trust and hope that if God intends me to rise he will open the way for me. Perhaps the very struggles and sorrows of a poor genius may teach him more than ever wealth and prosperity could.

Mr. C. True, Alton, my boy, and that's my only comfort. It does make men of us, this bitter battle of life. We workingmen, when we do come out of the furnace, come out steel and granite, and woe to the *papier-maché* gentleman that runs against us!

———◆———

METAPHYSICS.

Characters: TWO STUDENTS.

First. Pray tell me something about Metaphysics, for I cannot for my life make anything out of it.

Second. Metaphysics is the science of abstractions.

F. I am no wiser for that definition.

S. Well, take for example this earth. Now the earth may exist.

F. Who ever doubted that?

S. A great many men, and some very learned ones; although Bishop Berkeley has proved beyond all possible gainsaying or denial that it does not exist.

F. That is a point of considerable consequence to settle.

S. Now the earth may exist, and—

F. But how is all this to be found out?

S. By digging down to first principles.

F. Ay, there is nothing equal to the spade and pickaxe ; 'tis by digging that we can find out whether the world exists or not.

S. That is true, because if we dig to the bottom of the earth and find no foundation, then it is clear that the world stands upon nothing ; or, in other words, that it does not stand at all, therefore it stands to reason—

F. But if one can't believe his own eyes, what signifies talking about it ?

S. Our eyes are nothing but the inlets of sensation ; we are sure of nothing that we see with our eyes.

F. Well, what *does* a man begin to build upon in the metaphysical way ?

S. Why, he begins by taking something for granted.

F. But is that a sure way of going to work ?

S. Why it's—the—only thing he—can—do. Metaphysics is'the consideration of immateriality, or the mere spirit and essence of things. When we speak of essence of things, we mean the essence of locality, the essence of duration—

F. And the essence of peppermint ?

S. The essence I mean is quite a different affair. It is a thing that has no matter. It has no substance nor solidity, large nor small, hot nor cold, long nor short.

F. Then what is the long and short of it ?

S. Abstraction.

F. What do you say to a pitchfork as an abstraction ?

S. A pitchfork would mean none in particular, but one in general, and would be a thing in abstraction.

F. It would be a thing in the haymow. What do you think of a red cow for an example ?

S. A red cow, considered as an abstraction, would be an animal possessing neither hides nor horns, bones nor flesh ; it would have no color at all, for its redness would be the mere counterfeit or imagination of such.

It would neither go to pasture, chew cud, give milk, nor do anything of a like nature.

F. Nonsense! All the metaphysics under the sun wouldn't make a pound of butter!

———◆———

WORK: A STORY OF EXPERIENCE.

LOUISA M. ALCOTT.

[By permission of Roberts Bros.]

Characters: { Mrs. BETSY DEVON.
{ CHRISTIE DEVON, her niece.

C. D. Aunt Betsy, there's going to be a new Declaration of Independence.

Mrs. D. Bless us and save us! what do you mean, child?

C. D. I mean that, being of age, I'm going to take care of myself, and not be a burden any longer. Uncle thinks I ought to go away. I don't intend to wait for him to tell me so, but, like the people in fairy tales, travel away into the world and seek my fortune. I know I can find it.

Mrs. D. What crazy idee you got in your head now?

C. D. A very sane and sensible one, that's got to be worked out. I've had it a long time, and I've thought it over thoroughly, so I'm sure it's the right thing to do. I hate to be dependent, and, now there's no need of it, I can't bear it any longer. I'm old enough to take care of myself, and if I'd been a boy I should have been told to do it long ago. I'm sick of this dull town, where the one idea is, Eat, drink, and get rich; so let me go, Aunt Betsy, and find my place, wherever it is.

Mrs. D. You mustn't think your uncle don't like you. He does, only he don't show it. I don't see why you can't be contented. I've lived here all my days, and never found the place lonesome.

C. D. You and I are very different, ma'am. There was more yeast put into my composition, I guess; and after standing quiet in a warm corner so long, I begin to ferment, and ought to be kneaded up in time so that I may turn out a wholesome loaf, else I shall turn sour and good for nothing. Does that make the matter any clearer ?

Mrs. D. I see what you mean, Christie, but I never thought on't before. You be better riz than me; though, let me tell you, too much emptins makes bread poor stuff, like baker's trash; and too much workin' up makes it hard and dry. Now fly round, for the big oven is 'most hot, and this cake takes a sight of time in the mixin'.

C. D. You haven't said I might go, Aunt Betsy.

Mrs. D. (*Sorting ingredients and reading from cookbook*). I ain't no right to keep you, dear, if you choose to take (a pinch of salt). I'm sorry you ain't happy, and think you might be ef you'd only (beat six yolks and whites together). But if you can't, and feel that you need (two cups of sugar) only speak to your uncle, and ef he says (a squeeze of fresh lemon) go, my dear, and take my blessin' with you (not forgetting to cover with a piece of paper).

C. D. When I've done something to be proud of, you'll be glad to see me back again. Yes, I'll try my experiment; get rich; found a home for girls like myself; or, better still, be a Mrs. Fry, a Florence Nightingale, or—

Mrs. D. How are you on't for stockins', dear ?

C. D. Thank you for bringing me down to my feet again, when I was soaring away too far and too fast. I'm poorly off for stockings, ma'am.

Mrs. D. Don't you think you could be contented, Christie, ef I make the work lighter, and leave you more time for your books and things ?

C. D. No, ma'am, for I can't find what I want here.

Mrs. D. What *do* you want to find, child ?

C. D. Look in the fire and I'll try to show you. Do you see those two logs ? Well, that one smoldering dismally away in the corner is what my life is now; the other, blazing and singing, is what I want my life to be.

Mrs. D. Bless me, what an idee ! They are both a burnin' where they are put, and both will be ashes to-morrow; so what difference *does* it make ?

C. D. I know the end is the same; but it *does* make a difference *how* they turn to ashes, and *how* I spend my life. I hope my life, like the log which fills the room with light, may, whether long or short, be useful and cheerful while it lasts, will be missed when it ends, and leave something behind besides ashes.

Mrs. D. A good smart blowin' up with the belluses would make the green stick burn 'most as well as the dry one after a spell. I guess contentedness is the best bellus for young folks ef they would only think so.

C. D. I dare say you are right, Aunt Betsy, but I want to try for myself. If I fail, I'll come back and follow your advice.

NINETY-THREE.

Scene: A café in Paris. Time: June 28, 1793.

Characters:
{ ROBESPIERRE.
DANTON.
MARAT.

Danton. Listen! There is only one thing imminent—the peril of the Republic. I only know one thing—to deliver France from the enemy. To accomplish that all means are fair. Let us be terrible and useful. Does the elephant stop to look where he sets his foot? We must crush the enemy.

Robespierre. I shall be very glad. The question is to know where the enemy is.

Danton. It is outside, and I have chased it there.

Rob. It is within, and I watch it.

Marat. Calm yourselves. It is everywhere, and you are lost.

Rob. A truce to generalities. I particularize. Here are facts. In fifteen days they will have an army of brigands numbering three hundred thousand men, and all Brittany will belong to the King of France.

Marat. That is to say, to the King of England.

Rob. No, to the King of France. It needs fifteen days to expel the stranger, and eighteen hundred years to eliminate monarchy.

Danton. Very well, we will expel the English as we expelled the Prussians.

Rob. Sit down again, Danton, and look at the map, instead of knocking it with your fist.

Danton. That is madness! Robespierre, the danger is a circle, and we are within it. If this continue and we do not put things in order, the French Revolution will kill the King of France for the King of Prussia's sake.

Marat. You have each one his hobby. Danton, yours

is Prussia; Robespierre, yours is the Vendée. I am
going to state facts in my turn. You do not perceive
the real peril. It is the cafés and the gaming-houses.
It is the paper money, the famine, the stock-brokers,
and the monopolists—there is the danger. You see the
danger at a distance when it is close at hand. Yes, the
danger is everywhere, and above all in the centre.

Danton. There, there, there!

Marat. What is needed is a dictator. Robespierre,
you know that I want a dictator.

Rob. I know, Marat. You or me?

Marat. Me or you?

Danton. The dictatorship! Only try it!

Marat. Hold! One last effort. Let us get some
agreement. The situation is worth the trouble. Paris
must assume the government of the Revolution. So be
it. Well, the conclusion is a dictatorship. Let us seize
the dictatorship—we three who represent the Revolution. We are the three heads of Cerberus. Of these
three heads, one talks—that is you, Rebespierre; one
roars—that is you, Danton.

Danton. The other bites—that is you, Marat.

Rob. All three bite.

Marat. Ah, Robespierre! Ah, Danton! You will not
listen to me! Well, you are lost; I tell you so. You do
things which shut every door against you—except that
of the tomb.

Danton. That is our grandeur.

Marat. Danton, beware! Ah, you shrug your shoulders! Sometimes a shrug of the shoulders makes the
head fall. And as for thee, Robespierre, go on, powder
thyself, dress thy hair, brush thy clothes, play the cox-
comb. Fine as thou art, thou wilt be dragged at the
tails of four horses!

Rob. Echo of Coblentz !

Danton. I am the echo of nothing—I am the cry of the whole, Robespierre.

Marat. Ah, you are young, you ! How old art thou, Danton ? Four-and-thirty. How many are your years, Robespierre ? Thirty-three. Well, I—I have lived always. I am the old human suffering—I have lived six thousand years.

Danton. That is true. For six thousand years Cain has been preserved in hatred like the toad in a rock; the rock breaks, Cain springs out among men, and is called Marat.

Marat. Danton !

Danton. Marat talks very loud about the dictatorship and unity, but he has only one ability—that of breaking to pieces.

Rob. As for me, I say neither Roland nor Marat.

Marat. And I say neither Danton nor Robespierre. Let me give you advice, Danton. Do not meddle any more with politics—be wise. Adieu, gentlemen.

www.ingramcontent.com/pod-product-compliance
Lightning Source LLC
Chambersburg PA
CBHW020849270326
41928CB00006B/612